S0-AHG-420

When

F.D.R.

Died

When F.D.R. Died

BY BERNARD ASBELL

ILLUSTRATED WITH PHOTOGRAPHS

HOLT, RINEHART AND WINSTON · NEW YORK

Copyright © 1961 by Bernard Asbell

All rights reserved, including the right to reproduce
this book or portions thereof in any form.

Published simultaneously in Canada by Holt, Rinehart
and Winston of Canada, Limited.

First Edition

The author wishes to thank the following for permission
to use copyrighted material:

Harper & Brothers for material from *Thank You, Mr.
President* by A. Merriman Smith, copyright © 1946 by
A. Merriman Smith; and from *This I Remember* by Eleanor
Roosevelt, copyright © 1949 by Anna Eleanor Roosevelt.

Life for material from *Truman Memoirs* by Harry S. Truman;
copyright 1955, 1956, Time, Inc.

Pickwick Music Corporation, New York, New York, for lines
from "The Lonesome Train," text by Millard Lampell, music
by Earl Robinson. Copyright 1944, 1945 by Pickwick Music
Corporation.

Rutgers University Press for material from *Off the Record
with F.D.R.* by William D. Hassett, 1958.

Charles Scribner's Sons for material from *FDR, My Boss*
by Grace Tully, copyright © 1949 by Grace Tully.

Simon and Schuster, Inc., for material from *Reilly of the
White House*, by William J. Slocum and Michael F. Reilly;
copyright 1947 by William J. Slocum and Michael F. Reilly.

A portion of this book has appeared, in slightly different form,
in *Good Housekeeping* under the title, *F.D.R.: The Final Hours*.

Library of Congress Catalog Card Number: 61–9716

80533–0111

Designer: Ernst Reichl

Printed in the United States of America

To my wife,

Mildred.

We were together

when we heard the news.

Contents

Prologue

The weather was unseasonably warm along the Atlantic seaboard that afternoon. It was Thursday, April 12, 1945, a few minutes before six P.M.

That was when the news came.

Almost everyone remembers where he was when he heard the news . . . what he was doing . . . how he felt.

A soldier in Richmond, Virginia, on pass from a nearby Army hospital, was greeting his wife in front of a friend's house. A few yards away a little girl was bouncing a ball and reciting, in singsong, "Roosevelt's dead—Roosevelt's dead. . . ." First the soldier was appalled at the child's gruesome play. Then he was uneasy. He went into the house and turned on the radio. ". . . cerebral hemorrhage . . ." a voice was saying. ". . . the Little White House at Warm Springs. . . ." The soldier ran outside and exclaimed to his wife, "My God, it's true!"

At that moment, in the hold of a troop ship steaming into the port of Cherbourg, a crowd of young battle replacements was sitting on the floor, quiet, expectant, moving ever closer to the action of world war. A soldier strolled in and announced to no one in particular, "Guess what. The radio room says Roosevelt's dead." A few heads turned. "Good," someone said, "let's turn around and go home. We got no commander." The others laughed, and the subject was dropped. A few minutes later, an officer appeared at the door. "I have an announcement to make," he said. "The President—President Roosevelt has just died. We just got the word. . . ." He started to say more, but abruptly turned and left. There was an awful silence. A teen-age infantryman whispered, "But the war's almost over. . . ." After a moment of reflection, another boy said, "It's like somebody dying in your own family."

Many people felt such an intimate loss. Jonathan Daniels, who had just been appointed President Roosevelt's press secretary, was sitting in his small White House office chatting with Judge Anna M. Rosenberg when another Presidential secretary, Steve Early, burst in with the news. Daniels recalls how he felt: "It was like—just as though he told me my father died."

The wife of a garment manufacturer in New York was at home, hoping against hope that a certain call would not come. Her father was in a hospital, dying. The phone did ring and she heard the deeply sad voice of her brother, who had been waiting at the hospital. But he was saying something strange: ". . . terrible news. President Roosevelt just died." The woman felt first a wave of relief, then her whole world seemed to shake. Soon after, she began to cry. Her emotions were all confused. Her father was alive—but she *felt* as though a father had died.

In every direction, to the low and to the high, the word flashed. In Washington, D.C., Henry A. Wallace, the Secretary of Commerce and former Vice-President, was sitting in a dentist's chair when the telephone rang. The call was for Mr. Wallace from the White House. He took the phone and listened to the incredible words that eighty-three days earlier would have caused him to become President of the United States. He departed immediately for an emergency meeting of the Cabinet.

That was sixteen years ago. The death of Franklin Delano Roosevelt is now an old fact. Yet many people still cannot look back to the moment when the news came without feeling a subtle chill, a shadow of the first disbelief. A woman in Milwaukee says that when she heard the news it was like the banging of bass drums; she hears the drums again whenever someone mentions the time that Roosevelt died.

The dominant emotion, when the flash first came, was not sorrow but fear. Roosevelt had become, in twelve years of economic crisis and war, the towering personification of American government. Young people, who had not really known any other president, could hardly imagine national life without him. Older citizens felt, at the moment the flash came, the abrupt disintegration of an era. They had seen times change before; but never had they known an era to blow up and disappear between one instant and the next. The most commanding figure of the century suddenly was gone, and no one was prepared to contemplate what was to come.

"The greatness of Franklin Roosevelt," wrote Anne O'Hare McCormick on the day he died, "was indefinable while he lived because it was a compound of many qualities, including the qualities of smaller men—and also because he did not make a point of it. No one was more aware that among the leaders of his time he occupied a great position as President of the United States, a role so fused with his own personality after twelve years that people in other countries spoke of him simply as 'The President,' as if he were the President of the world. But he did not pose as a great man. If he posed at all, it was not as somebody on an eminence, but as one who lived comfortably on all levels, a human being to whom nothing human was alien. He did not stoop and he did not climb; he was one of those completely poised persons who felt no need to play up or play down to anybody.

"In his death this is the element of his greatness that comes out most clearly."

When

F.D.R.

Died

I

"Do You Believe in Reincarnation?"

In the early morning mist of April 12, 1945, atop Pine Mountain near Warm Springs, Georgia, important things were cooking: two 150-pound hogs and a 100-pound lamb. Droplets of melted fat sizzled over an open-pit fire, spreading an inviting aroma across the pine-straw lawn of Frank Allcorn, the Mayor of Warm Springs and owner of its small hotel.

The Mayor of the tiny village was taking the whole day off—on a Thursday—to throw a country barbecue. In a huge iron pot were the makings of a Brunswick stew; on his guest list, the makings of a great day. At the top of the guest list was the President of the United States.

A bony-featured woman with close-cropped hair, intense eyes, and staccato gestures scurried about, tasting something here, moving a chair there, and calling an occasional order to Mr. Allcorn or her Warm Springs neighbors, Jess Long and Leonard Williams. Ruth Stevens, the manager of the Warm Springs Hotel, was clearly running this show. Since five in the morning she had cooked twelve five-pound hens, two hogs' heads, eighteen cans of tomatoes, eighteen cans of corn, and twenty-five pounds of beef. All of these were to be served, starting at 4 P.M., at what was to be the most overwhelming social event of her life.

She directed Allcorn, Long, and Williams in grouping green-and-white lawn chairs and hammocks under the hickory nut trees. They arranged tables in the shape of an immense U, and covered them with oilcloth. Mrs. Stevens selected a green wooden armchair with a fat cushion made of silk scraps. She set it down at the opening of the U. This would be for the President. She prettied up the tables with clusters of wild white azaleas and sprays of green huckleberry. She set out oval bowls for Brunswick stew and barbecue, and smaller Mexican bowls for potato chips. Around a two-hundred-year-old coffeepot, she arranged a set of brown crockery mugs.

As the morning warmed with the promise of a midday glow, a detail of men from the United States Secret Service drove up. While they joked with Mrs. Stevens, they went about the serious business of running their hands under the furniture and peering behind every bush. One of them asked Mrs. Stevens which chair the President would sit in. He then fingered it like a blind man. The President's chauffeur, Monty Snyder, arrived in a big White House Lincoln. He rehearsed moving the car into the Allcorn driveway. Major DeWitt Greer of the United States Army Signal Corps showed up with a detachment of his men. They set up a short-wave station in the barn.

While these early morning preparations were being made, Chief Petty Officer Graham Jackson of the United States Coast Guard was struggling with his automobile on U.S. Route 80, west of Macon—struggling to keep the car down to the wartime speed limit of thirty-five miles an hour. Jackson, a squarely built Negro, whose bald head crouched like a boulder between two mountainous shoulders, was by nature a man in a hurry. He was especially so now.

Jackson was an entertainer—piano, accordian, and voice —who was sometimes described as Franklin D. Roosevelt's favorite musician, a distinction he was too modest to confirm but too honest to deny. The fact of the matter was that whenever Mr. Roosevelt came to Warm Springs, Jackson could expect a summons to entertain. He had received such a summons only yesterday, an invitation to take part in a minstrel show for the patients of the Georgia Warm Springs Foundation.

The Foundation had been started by Roosevelt in 1927 to enable thousands of polio victims to strengthen their withered limbs, as he had done, in the warm waters of natural springs. On the grounds, Roosevelt had built a vacation cottage for himself. The cottage, which was to become known as the Little White House, was secluded, but close enough to the center of Foundation activities so Roosevelt could easily take part in them. He planned, in fact, to attend the dress rehearsal of the patients' minstrel show right after the barbecue at Frank Allcorn's, where he would once again enjoy the talents of Graham Jackson.

At the center of the Foundation, in a small tree-shaded dwelling called Carver Cottage, a telephone rang a few minutes after eight A.M. This cottage was occupied by William D. Hassett, the Secretary to the President, and two agreeable ladies, Miss Grace Tully, the President's private secretary, and Mrs. Dorothy Brady, the assistant to Miss Tully. Hassett had made a deal with the girls. He was given exclusive rights to the cottage's single bathroom until eight, after which it was all theirs. Having just emerged from the bathroom, Hassett answered the phone. A caller from Washington informed him that the President's mail would be delayed. It usually arrived in Warm Springs at nine. But today it would not get there until almost noon, because bad weather in Washington had locked the courier plane to the land.

The news meant that the morning would be for loafing. Hassett, a gentle-mannered Vermonter with silver-rimmed spectacles, was glad. He assured himself that the cause of the free world would be well served this morning by having Franklin Delano Roosevelt stay in bed. The Boss needed it.

With Grace Tully, Hassett replanned the President's day. Since the Boss would catch extra winks in the morning, he could skip his nap after lunch. Then he would start dictating to Grace the first draft of his speech to the conference in San Francisco thirteen days hence, where the United Nations would be born. A good chunk of the job could be accomplished before the afternoon barbecue and the minstrel show that night.

Then Hassett called the Little White House, about a third of a mile away in a secluded clearing of mountain woods, to send word of the revised schedule.

Since the President would be taking the morning off, so would his staff. Miss Tully and Mrs. Brady decided the late morning would be a good time for a dip and a sun bath at what was known as the "patient's pool." Miss Tully picked up her bedroom phone and invited the chief White House telephone operator, Miss Louise Hachmeister, who was performing her duties at a switchboard in a bedroom of a nearby cottage. Hacky readily accepted. The girls also invited Commander Howard G. Bruenn, a forty-year-old Navy doctor charged with protecting the President's health. Bruenn had been sent to Warm Springs by Rear Admiral

Ross T. McIntire, the Navy Surgeon General who was also the President's personal physician.

In the Little White House, a six-room clapboard cottage with a four-column portico at its entrance, a curious conversation was taking place.

"Do you believe in reincarnation?"

The question, asked by Joe Esperancilla, a Filipino houseboy, was addressed to Lizzie McDuffie, a grandmotherly Negro maid. They were frittering away the quiet morning in the old-fashioned kitchen, sitting and eating at a wooden work-table beneath a bare electric bulb that dangled from a long wire.

Lizzie peered at Joe, trying to probe the hidden intent of the question. "I don't know if I believe in it or not," she said. "But if there is such a thing, when I come back to this world I want to be a canary bird."

Joe laughed. "And I suppose you'll sit in a cage and eat all the time."

Lizzie was indignant. At every opportunity—no matter what she said—they teased her about her incessant eating. She stomped out of the kitchen and into the entry area of the cottage, and began to dust. She whisked her duster over a simple drop-leaf table, along the cracks between the pine panels of the walls, around the panes of window glass that rose from the floor.

She glided into the large central room, a combined living room and dining area. Cheery sunlight poured between the slats of green-blue Venetian blinds hanging from ceiling to floor. Turning to her right, she skimmed the bookshelves that lined the wall beside a worn, puffy sofa. Then she dusted the model of a Nantucket whaler above a great stone fireplace. Crossing into the dining area, she puttered over a maple table, six handcrafted straight-backed chairs, an old-fashioned Dutch sideboard displaying cocktail glasses and knickknacks, and marine wall decorations. These were near a plank door that was standing open.

Through the doorway there boomed a resonant voice, subtly shaded with severity.

"Lizzie! You all have been having a *grand* time out there."

Lizzie gasped. She glanced toward the kitchen. Her conversation with Joe must have been much too loud.

"Oh my. I wonder, did we disturb you? I'm awful sorry."

"Oh no, no," the voice said, the severity melting away. "But what in the world were you laughing about?"

Lizzie was now at the door. The President of the United States was sitting in bed, the corners of his pillow sticking out behind his head like rabbit's ears. He was holding a newspaper. But his head was tilted back, eyes lit for engagement in conversation.

"Well, Mr. Roosevelt," Lizzie ventured, "do you believe in reincarnation?"

"Do I believe in *what?*"

"Reincarnation."

As she had often overheard him do with others, he threw the question back at the questioner: "Well tell me, do *you* believe in reincarnation?"

"I don't know if I do or not. But that's what Joe was trying to find out when you heard all that fuss. I told him I don't know, but in case there is such a thing, when I come back I want to be a canary bird."

The scene is etched clearly in Mrs. McDuffie's memory: "He looked at me from head to foot—I weighed about two hundred pounds then—and he burst out into *peals* of laughter and just threw his paper down. Such laughter you never heard. He looked at how fat I was and said, 'A canary bird!' Well, the President had a favorite word he always said when anything amused him. He'd say, 'Don't you love it? Don't you *love* it?' And that's just what he said then.

"Mr. Roosevelt always had time to lay down what he was doing and just talk to you. He always had time if you wanted to ask him about the meaning of something. He would draw you out, you know. He'd ask, 'Why do you want to know this?' Sometimes I'd say, 'Well, I just thought probably you knew more about it.' And then he'd laugh in that way of his and say, 'Aw, I don't know any more about it than you do.' "

Lizzie asked the President how he was feeling.

"Oh, I don't feel any too good this morning, Lizzie."

He placed his palm on the back of his neck and worked his head this way and that. The President's sinuses sometimes caused mild headaches in the morning, but Mrs. McDuffie could not recall a previous time when he had ever indicated a headache in the back of his head.

Mrs. McDuffie changed the subject.

"Those waffles you had last night, do you know they were made on the waffle iron Mr. Morgenthau gave you last Christmas?"

"Yes, I know," Mr. Roosevelt said. "That's probably why old Henry enjoyed those waffles so much."

It was not entirely a change of subject. A visit the previous evening by Secretary of the Treasury Morgenthau had been the occasion for Mrs. McDuffie to engage in another conversation about the President's health. She was in the kitchen, eating. The President was sitting outside, awaiting the arrival of his dinner guest.

Daisy Bonner, the cook, was looking out the window. Daisy said thoughtfully: "Lizzie, don't you think the President looks feeble?"

Lizzie said, "Yes, I think the President looks feeble. But he does look better than he did when he first came."

"I know what I'm going to do," Daisy said. "I'm going to give him the things he *likes* to eat, regardless of the doctor and what all those people say." She enumerated certain things he especially liked: turnip greens; hush puppies; and Daisy's specialty, Country Captain, a form of curried chicken.

Often Daisy and Lizzie had whispered grumpily in the kitchen about the things other people tried to make the President eat. Daisy would say to Lizzie: "You tell him we're going to have so-and-so-and-so for dinner, and you tell him that I say don't eat any."

Then Lizzie would steal up to the President before dinner and whisper, "Daisy says when dinner is served don't eat so-and-so-and-so."

"All right," the President would say quietly, "I won't."

And he wouldn't. Margaret Suckley or Laura Delano, the President's cousins who had accompanied him to Warm Springs, might say, "Franklin, aren't you going to eat what Daisy made?" He'd say, "Oh, I'll eat some of that tomorrow."

Despite the President's complaint of a headache, Lizzie thought he did look well this morning. In the morning, he always looked his best.

Now he had turned back to reading the Atlanta *Constitution*, which had come with his breakfast tray. His usual four papers, the New York *Times*, New York *Herald Tribune*, Baltimore *Sun*, and Washington *Post*, had been delayed in Washington with the mail. So, with no work to do and only one newspaper, the President read with leisure.

The headline was not entirely news to the Commander in Chief, but it was good to see:

9TH 57 MILES FROM BERLIN
50-MILE GAIN IN DAY
SETS STAGE FOR EARLY
U.S.-RUSS JUNCTURE

PARIS, Thursday, April 12 (AP)—Armored columns of the
U.S. Ninth Army swept within 57 miles of Berlin and within
115 miles of the Russian front yesterday in a startling advance
of more than 50 miles that carried to the Elbe river at Magde-
burg. A crossing of this last water barrier before the German
capital was believed imminent. . . .

There was also good news from the Pacific:

150 SUPERFORTS HAMMER TOKYO
IN TWO-HOUR DAYLIGHT RAID

In addition to what the Commander already knew, there
were the beginnings of rumors—highly untrustworthy, to
be sure, but worth watching:

LONDON, April 11 (AP)—The British press reported without confirmation today that Adolf Hitler, broken in health,
and perhaps dying, has been forced by the Nazis to yield control over the toppling Reich to Heinrich Himmler.
Foreign Secretary Anthony Eden was asked in Commons
whether he could confirm a report that Hitler had been assas-
sinated, but he brushed it aside in a manner indicating he
gave it no credence.
The London newspapers amplified a report issued by the
British Press Association which said its diplomatic correspondent has authoritative information that Hitler already
has been superseded by Himmler and that Hitler is "a dying
man."

Mr. Roosevelt thumbed through the inside pages. There
was yesterday's announcement from Washington of the

cold and imponderable statistics: the war to date had cost
the lives of 196,669 Americans. The total casualties—
killed, wounded, and missing—were 899,390. This represented an increase of 6,481 over the figure a week ago.

Nowhere in the paper did he find mention of the man he
most enjoyed reading about—himself. The paper didn't
even publish the routine "announcements" the President
was supposed to have made in Washington the day before.
Such announcements were one form of wartime camou-
flage to reinforce a natural assumption that he was in the
White House when actually he was off on a secret trip.
But a report on the last page from the official seat of government was worth a chuckle. Poor old Alben Barkley,
the trusty and eloquent majority leader of the Senate,
seemed to be having trouble on his hands. His troops were
in revolt:

Rebellious Ellender
Skips—Hey, Barkley

Washington, April 11 (AP)—Sen. Ellender, Democrat,
Louisiana, headed home today, a little rebellious about the
verbal rock-throwing that went on under the Senate's glass
dome. . . .

The doughty little Louisianan's feathers were ruffled yesterday when Democratic Leader Barkley, Kentucky, jumped
on his colleagues for staying away from the Senate in droves
when important legislation is under consideration.

Ellender jumped up to say that Barkley had told the Senate
the Mexican water treaty was going to be discussed for a
couple of weeks. That's why he was going home, Ellender
added, and that probably was why a lot of senators were not
there.

Mr. Roosevelt looked at his watch. It was after eleven.
The mail would soon be here and an artist was coming to
paint his portrait. He folded his newspaper and put it down

on a bed table next to a paper-bound book, lying open and face down, that he had been reading the night before. It was *The Punch and Judy Murders*, one in a series of Sir Henry Merrivale mysteries, by Carter Dickson, a pseudonym of John Dickson Carr. The macabre discovery was made later in the day by Mr. Roosevelt's valet, Arthur Prettyman, that the book was opened to page seventy-eight, the beginning of a chapter entitled "Six Feet of Earth."

2

"I Never
Believed He'd Die"

For almost two weeks now, the mind of C. A. Pless had been, in the faintest sort of way, uneasy. Mr. Pless was the station agent at the tiny peaked-roof railroad depot beside the Warm Springs Hotel. The hours between trains were long and many. Therefore, Mr. Pless, sitting by a wood stove chewing a cud of tobacco and spitting its juice into a can, could take more time than most people to contemplate the subtle signs of an ever-changing world outside his depot window.

President Roosevelt had arrived at Mr. Pless's depot during the afternoon of Good Friday, March 30th, as he had done almost every spring and autumn during his twelve years in the presidency. But this arrival, in one respect, was not like the others, and that was what was troubling the station agent. This time, when the presidential special halted by the depot, Mr. Roosevelt didn't break out with his big grin and start waving to everybody. He didn't wave at all.

Dozens of neighbors were there, a big crowd for a village of six hundred. Ruth Stevens and Frank Allcorn, of course, were among the crowd. So was Mabel Irwin, the wife of the Foundation's chief surgeon, and Neal Kitchens, the eighty-six-year old country doctor to whose home the President had once come for dinner. There was Minnie Bulloch, owner of the general store, and Turnley Walker, a writer who had been stricken by polio and was now a patient at the Foundation. They watched the President in his wheel chair descending on the tiny elevator built into the rear platform of his observation car. His big figure was slumped, his hat pulled low. He didn't seem to see the crowd.

"The President was the worst-looking man I ever saw who was still alive," Mr. Pless has said. "Just like a setting up dead man."

From a forward car Merriman Smith, the United Press White House correspondent, stepped down and joined the crowd. Ruth Stevens seized his arm.

"Honey, is he *all right?*"

"Tired to death," Smith said. "But he'll pull out of it. He always does."

Allcorn stepped forward. "Welcome home, Mr. President."

Roosevelt's head tilted up and for the first time his face warmed. "Why, His Honor the Mayor." He lifted his hand toward the brim of his floppy hat. The hand brushed his pince-nez glasses and knocked them off. A Secret Service man stooped at once to pick them up. Roosevelt, impatiently, pinched them back in place.

Mr. Pless could not recall ever seeing Mr. Roosevelt not waving if there were someone to wave to.

"I remember the time he was driving by the station—himself at the wheel—and he saw a colored man walking by that crossroads. The President waved him over to talk.

The colored man was scared, scraping his feet and all, just answering 'yes sir' and 'no sir.' Then first thing you know, he was leaning on the President's automobile, throwing his arms around like he was talking to anybody. To Roosevelt, it didn't make any difference if your overalls had a seat in them or not. If he figured you were a farmer or worked for a living, he cared about you. He was always setting people at their ease, getting them close to him."

To the couple of hundred families of Warm Springs, Roosevelt was more than a President who frequently honored them by his presence. He was a neighbor, participating in their community life. Some folks in the station crowd remembered the night in the '20s when Roosevelt had come to a town meeting boiling mad. He had just received his electric bill. The rate was eighteen cents a kilowatt hour, almost four times what he was paying at Hyde Park, New York. At the meeting he marshaled a committee to go to the electric company and protest. But the committee got nowhere. Then Roosevelt learned that hundreds of outlying farm houses, despite the high rates, could not get wired for electricity at all.

Years later, on May 11, 1935, when Roosevelt signed into law the Rural Electrification Act, it was a proud day for the village. The President told the whole country that his experience at Warm Springs "started my long study of proper utility charges for electricity and the whole subject of getting electricity into farm houses throughout the United States."

So to the people at the station now troubled by his look of weariness, Roosevelt was not only a world figure but a good neighbor as well. The villagers returned the devotion. Only a few months before his last arrival at Warm Springs, when Roosevelt ran for a fourth consecutive term, only 181 residents of Meriwether County voted for his op-

ponent, Thomas E. Dewey; 3,187 marked their ballots for
F.D.R.

The people of Warm Springs, although disturbed by the
President's bad appearance when he arrived, did not seriously worry about it for long. Together with many people
of other places, they had heard so much false speculation
about the President's health, that they were largely im-
mune to the subject.

As far back as 1932, when Roosevelt was fifty and
running for President for the first time, whispers were
widespread that his battle against infantile paralysis had
drained him and that he was about to die. The whispers
spread again eight years later when Roosevelt broke tradition by seeking a third term; it was rumored that Roosevelt was an aging cripple, surrounded by conspirators who
concealed the true state of his health. These rumors were
revived in December, 1943, when the President returned
from meeting Winston Churchill and Joseph Stalin at Teheran.

Such whispers were not entirely without foundation.
Reporters at Roosevelt's press conferences found his voice
weak; often they had to repeat their questions because the
President didn't quite hear; his shipboard tan faded faster
than usual. Admiral McIntire explained to the press that
Roosevelt's sinuses were acting up. In the winter of 1944,
Roosevelt found it necessary to slip off for a month's rest
at Bernard Baruch's South Carolina estate.

As autumn approached, the lingering concern for his
health accentuated an urgent question of the year: Would
Roosevelt run for a fourth term? His enemies could hardly
believe he would dare. His friends could hardly believe he
would decline. Roosevelt said nothing.

Under the demands of war, Roosevelt canceled many
press conferences. Newsmen, seeing less of the President,

couldn't help but be more responsive to rumors. An epidemic of reports broke out in 1944 that Roosevelt had been spirited away for a serious operation. Merriman Smith picked up two persistent tales: one, that he was in a hospital in Boston; the other, that he was at the Mayo clinic in Rochester, Minnesota. The Mayo rumor, as it came to Smith, even included the President's suite number and the names of his doctors and nurses. Smith, checking out both tales, found nothing to support them. But they were disconcerting.

Roosevelt himself was not unmindful of the rumors, nor indifferent. During the campaign he became angered by them. Touring New York City during a merciless rain, he insisted on waving at the crowds from an open car. Early in the evening, he stopped to change clothes at an apartment near Washington Square. It was a place that his wife had quietly rented for their visits to New York City after they finally departed the White House. This was the only visit Roosevelt ever made to the flat. That day he had spoken at Ebbets Field, Brooklyn, standing bareheaded in a cold, driving rain. Next day at Hyde Park, while members of his party were laid low with sniffles, Roosevelt laughed and said he felt fine.

But the toughest ten days of Roosevelt's life were still ahead. In February, 1945—after his fourth inauguration— he left on a secret trip to meet again with Churchill and Stalin, this time at Yalta in the Crimea. It required arduous travel, and a week of arduous discussion. They plotted the culminating strategy for victory in Europe, divided the areas of postwar influence, timed the entrance of Russia into the war against Japan, and touched up the blueprint for a permanent United Nations organization. This was not like previous Big Three meetings. Earlier, the war leaders had pooled their thoughts toward a common end: defeating the enemy. Now they found themselves grappling over the spoils of a victory at hand. Each brought his country's vision of a postwar arrangement; each buttressed his vision with a record of national sacrifice. Each pressed, yet each held back, because there was still a war to win; they still needed one another.

On Roosevelt's return voyage aboard the U.S.S. *Quincy* through submarine-infested waters, the three press association reporters permitted to accompany him saw more of the President than they had ever seen in a short period. "It seemed," Merriman Smith was later to write, "he had aged ten years in ten days. He sat all day in the sun. . . . He had lost weight, but he refused to take it seriously, said he would gain it back at Warm Springs."

Two days out of Algiers, Roosevelt suffered a grievous personal blow. Major General Edwin M. Watson, his appointment secretary, died on shipboard. The bond between "Pa" Watson and the Boss transcended their official relationship. Pa was a raconteur and a good listener, a confidant and laughing partner. But the President was forced to swallow his grief, laboring on deck with Judge Samuel I. Rosenman over a report to a joint session of Congress.

On Thursday, March 1st, the chamber and galleries of the House of Representatives were packed and astir. It was plain something unusual was to take place. A table laden with microphones stood in the well of the chamber, little more than an arm's length from the first curved row of seats. For the first time, the President was to speak to a live audience while sitting down. And for the first time, he was to make public mention of his disability.

"Mr. Vice-President, Mr. Speaker, and members of the Congress," he began slowly, looking around. His face was drawn, and there were ominous dark patches beneath his eyes. A weariness was in his voice that his audience had not heard before. Then the President said, extemporaneously, "I hope that you will pardon me for the unusual posture of sitting down during the presentation of what I want to say, but I know that you will realize it makes it a lot easier for me in not having to carry about ten pounds of steel around on the bottom of my legs, and also because of the fact that I have just completed a fourteen-thousand-mile trip. . . . I am returning from this trip that took me so far, refreshed and inspired. I was well the entire time. I was not ill for a second until I arrived back in Washington and here I heard all the rumors which had occurred in my absence. Yes, I returned from the trip refreshed and inspired. The Roosevelts are not, as you may suspect, averse to travel. We seem to thrive on it."

After weeks away from his desk, the papers demanding attention were piled high. Roosevelt began to do what he had previously promised Admiral McIntire he would no longer do. He lunched at his desk from a rolling steam table; every lunch was the scene of a conference. He had agreed, under McIntire's demand, to take naps after lunch; now he stopped taking them. He often skipped his daily rubdown, and worked far into the night. Still, McIntire found no specific symptoms of organic ailment; only the obvious signs of fatigue and a loss of about fifteen pounds from his normal range of 184 to 188. McIntire advised Roosevelt to take a month at Warm Springs. Instead, the President sought rest during weekends at Hyde Park. On one weekend, the President suffered a gastrointestinal upset that put him off his usual diet. Finally, he consented to go to Warm Springs.

On the morning of March 29th, Roosevelt arrived in Washington from Hyde Park. He was to leave for Warm Springs in a few hours. Grace Tully saw at a glance that the weekend at home had failed to erase the fatigue from the President's face. At one o'clock, the President left his office for lunch. At three he was to see Archibald MacLeish, the Assistant Secretary of State, and Jonathan Daniels, the White House press secretary. They needed the President's approval of an urgent statement. Miss Tully has recalled the meeting:

"We had been waiting for the Boss in the Oval Study, and when he was wheeled in I was so startled I almost burst into tears. In two hours he seemed to have failed dangerously. His face was ashen, highlighted by the darkening shadows under his eyes and with cheeks drawn gauntly. Both Daniels and MacLeish looked at him closely and I could see that they also were struck by his appearance. They showed him the proposed statement, however, and drew him carefully into a discussion of its meaning and exact wording. He read it with evident care but suggested only some minor changes before indicating his approval."

The text approved by the President began:

"Soviet representatives at the Yalta Conference indicated their desire to raise at the San Francisco Conference of the United Nations the question of representation for the Ukrainian Soviet Republic and the White Russian Soviet Republic in the assembly of the proposed United Nations organization. The American and British representatives at the Yalta Conference were requested by the Soviet representatives to support this proposal when submitted to the conference of the United Nations at San Francisco. They agreed to do so, but the American representatives stated that if the United Nations organization agreed to let the Soviet Republics have three votes, the United States would ask for three votes also. . . ."

Miss Tully then handed Mr. Roosevelt a legislative bill bearing a red tab, meaning "urgent." She told him he could sign all the other papers at Warm Springs. Ordinarily, he protested the postponement of signing papers, lest they pile up. This time he wearily, almost gratefully, agreed.

Then Miss Tully put before the President a bound copy of a prayer he had written for D-Day. She thought he might like to sign it for his grandson, Johnny Boettiger, who was in a hospital with an infected throat. The President wrote a cheering message on the flyleaf. It was the last time he was to sign his name in the White House.

Next day at the Warm Springs railroad depot, while Station Agent Pless was noting unhappily that the President didn't wave, an equally individual observation disturbed the chief of the Secret Service detail, Michael F. Reilly:

"It was no premonition of death, because I never believed he'd die. . . . But I knew something was wrong. . . . The business of transferring the President into a car was usually pretty simple. . . . He'd reach backwards until his hands had secured a firm grip on each side of the car door, and then he'd actually surge out of your arms into the car and onto the jump seat. Then he'd reach back once more and pull himself to the rear seat of the car. He did this with such speed and grace that literally thousands who had seen him at ball games, rallies, and inaugurations never suspected his condition. . . . But it took every bit of strength I could muster to make the transfer that evening at Warm Springs. He was absolutely dead weight. . . . I passed the word on to the Detail that the Boss was 'heavy,' and I told Commander Howard Bruenn. . . ."

While everyone around the President was disturbed by the signs, only one man in the official family is known to have stated his fears. Bill Hassett, standing that night with Dr. Bruenn before the tall columns of Georgia Hall on the Foundation grounds, unburdened himself of certain private thoughts. A few minutes after the conversation, he reconstructed it in his diary. The entry reads:

"Tonight had another talk with Howard Bruenn about the President's health. I said: 'He is slipping away from us and no earthly power can keep him here.' Bruenn demurred. 'Why do you think so?' he asked. Told him I understood his position—his obligation to save life, not to admit defeat. Then I reminded him that I gave him the same warning when we were here last December. He remembered. I said: 'I know you don't want to make the admission and I have talked this way with no one else save one. To all his staff, to the family, and with the Boss himself I have maintained the bluff; but I am convinced there is no help for him.' Bruenn very serious. We were both on the verge of emotional upset. He asked to whom I had talked. I hesitated to answer. He guessed right: Doc O'Connor [Basil O'Connor, Roosevelt's former law partner and lifelong friend]. I told him Doc and I had come to that conviction before election. He wanted to know how long I had had this feeling. I told him for a year, but worried particularly because of the Boss's indifference after the Chicago convention—didn't act like a man who cared a damn about the election. Then he got mad at Dewey for the low level on which he pitched his campaign and came back strong at the All-American Boy in the Statler Speech before Dan Tobin's teamsters last September.

"Then F.D.R. got his Dutch up. That did the trick. He got madder and madder over Dewey's technique. That was the turning point to my mind. Despite even the exposure of that campaign tour through New York City in a cold October rain, which he completed without contracting a cold or even a sniffle, I could not but notice his increasing weariness as I handled his papers with him, particularly at Hyde Park, trip after trip. He was always willing to go through the day's routine, but there was less and less talk about all manner of things—fewer local Hyde Park stories, politics, books, pictures. The old zest was going.

"I told Bruenn I had every confidence in his own skill; was satisfied that the Boss was the beneficiary of everything that the healing art can devise. I couldn't suggest anything which should be done differently, but in my opin-

ion the Boss was beyond all human resources. I mentioned
his feeble signature—the old boldness of stroke and liberal
use of ink gone, signature often ending in a fade-out. He
said that not important. Reluctantly admitted the Boss in a
precarious condition, but his condition not hopeless. He
could be saved if measures were adopted to rescue him
from certain mental strains and emotional influences, which
he mentioned. I told him his conditions could not be met
and added that this talk confirmed my conviction that the
Boss is leaving us.

"When we separated in front of Georgia Hall, I felt that
the doctor shared the layman's point of view. Bruenn is a
man of superior intellect and integrity—in short, a gentleman of highest attainment in his profession. He would inspire anyone's confidence. All things considered, it was
difficult for me to speak as I did. We said good night with
heavy hearts."

Hassett felt unburdened, but not relieved. Next night,
he wrote in his diary:

"Shocked at his appearance—worn, weary, exhausted.
He seemed all right when I saw him in the morning. He is
steadily losing weight—told me he has lost twenty-five
pounds—no strength, no appetite, tires so easily—all too
apparent whenever you see him after midday. Again observed all this to Dr. Bruenn. He admits cause for alarm."

And again the next night, Sunday, April 1st, Hassett put
into his diary private, unspeakable fears that, it seemed, no
one else shared:

"Easter Day. To the Foundation Chapel this morning
with an overpowering sense of last things." And he added:
"If I remember rightly, it was on Easter Day six years ago
that we left for Washington and the Boss from the rear
platform of the car made the famous crack: 'I'll be back in
the fall if we don't have a war.' Alas for the misery of the
years since."

Three other men in the Presidential party were watchful for signs of the President's health, not so much because they were apprehensive but because there was little else they could fruitfully watch. These were the three press association reporters. They had been permitted to come to Warm Springs on the understanding that no news would be released to them and they could dispatch none. As far as the country and the world knew, the President was still in Washington.

The reporters were Merriman Smith of United Press, a raspy voiced fast talker with a pencil-thin mustache and the fun-loving instincts of a resort social director; D. Harold Oliver of Associated Press, a wiry man with a high, soft voice and an unobtrusive, efficient manner which seemed to blend with the gentle aura of Warm Springs; and Robert G. Nixon of International News Service, who, as an employee of William Randolph Hearst, was obliged to regard Roosevelt in the public print with a cool and distant eye, but who long ago had decided privately that Franklin Roosevelt was the most gracious man he had ever known.

During their first few days at Warm Springs, they golfed, slept late, and partied with the White House staff. But of official matters they heard nothing. They grew frustrated. They wanted to talk to the President. Even social chitchat would do. There was always a chance the President might tip off a problem that was on his complicated mind. If he did, the men might be free to write about it when they returned to Washington.

Six days after they arrived—on Thursday, April 5th— the reporters received a hurry-up call for a press conference and were admitted to the Little White House living room. Roosevelt was sitting in his brown leather armchair before the fireplace, the Georgia sunshine spilling through the blinds across his shoulders. In a corner, inconspicuously,

Dorothy Brady sat ready to take stenographic notes. The President's Scottie dog, Fala, waddled about, sniffing at trouser cuffs. Next to Roosevelt sat a tiny, dark, frail man. Roosevelt introduced him as Sergio Osmeña, the President of the Philippine Commonwealth. Osmeña smiled, nodding almost obsequiously, as Roosevelt began to speak:

"President Osmeña and I have been having a nice talk and I thought you could come up and write a story for release when we get back to Washington. It may be in another week or ten days. The President and I talked about many things, and it so happened that while we were together this morning, the announcement about the fall of the Japanese Cabinet was told. It is a piece of very good news. Outside of that, we have been talking about a great many things to do with the Philippines."

This was almost the whole truth. The fact was, however, that Roosevelt called the conference not so much to edify the press as to free himself gracefully of Osmeña. His plan, when he came to Warm Springs, was to receive no official visitors at all. Osmeña, however, about to be released from an American hospital after an operation, had transmitted urgent pleas to White House subordinates for a day of conferences with the American President. This was out of the question, but Roosevelt finally consented to give him a couple of hours. In the last minute, Roosevelt devised the press conference as a way of sending the little leader on his way, satisfied that he had addressed the world.

Merriman Smith noted that Roosevelt's hands seemed to tremble more than usual as he fitted a Camel cigarette into his famous stained holder and lit it with a kitchen match. It was an intense and uncomfortable thing to watch. As a victim of polio, Roosevelt often revealed a fluttering of the hands, but not quite so much as of late.

As always, however, Roosevelt moved to center stage and held it. (Even when he introduced Churchill to a press conference in Washington, Roosevelt did almost all the talking.) Without offering the floor to Osmeña, Roosevelt talked in detail about the destruction of Manila and guerrilla fighting in the countryside, the past and future of tariff agreements, plans for technical assistance and for safeguarding the whole Pacific against future aggression. Carefully, he restricted his discussion to the Philippines, to please Osmeña on the one hand and, on the other, to forestall a free-for-all inquiry on other questions. The reporters skillfully broached other questions anyhow.

"Mr. President," one reporter began, "you mentioned the collapse of the Japanese Cabinet. Do you think there is any connection between that and the Russian renunciation of the nonaggression pact with Japan?"

"I wouldn't know," Roosevelt said, lifting his brows playfully. "I would get into what you boys call the speculative field if I tried to answer."

Another reporter then questioned Osmeña about his travel plans, but the news-hungry group couldn't help but get back to more pressing matters. They were especially eager for a word from Roosevelt about the terse White House announcement a week earlier, agreeing to give the Soviet Union three votes in the United Nations General Assembly.

"Mr. President," a reporter ventured, "do you think we will have a chance to talk with you again on other subjects before you go, such as the three-to-one vote?"

"I think you will see me several times before I go. Some of the boys cannot get their facts straight. It would really be fun if I went on the air and simply read the things which have appeared in the paper. Of course, you know that it is not true factually."

The reporter, sensing success in his goading, said: "There certainly have been as many different interpretations as I have ever seen on anything."

Roosevelt suddenly looked as if he had something to say. The reporter had achieved his goal.

"As a matter of fact, this plea for votes was done in a very quiet way. Stalin said to me—and this is the essence of it—'You know, there are two parts of Russia that have been completely devastated. Every building is gone, every farmhouse, and there are millions of people living in these territories—and it is very important from the point of view of humanity—and we thought, as a gesture, they ought to be given something as a result of this coming victory. They have had very little civilization. One is the Ukraine, and the other is White Russia. We all felt—not any of us coming from there in the government—we think it would be grand to give them a vote in the Assembly. In these two sections, millions have been killed, and we think it would be very heartening—would help to build them up —if we could get them a vote in the Assembly.' He asked me what I thought.

"I said to Stalin, 'Are you going to make that request of the Assembly?' He said, 'I think we should.' I said, 'I think it would be all right—I don't know how the Assembly will vote.'

"He said, 'Would you favor it?' I said, 'Yes, largely on sentimental grounds. If I were on the delegation—which I am not—I would probably vote "yes." '

"That has not come out in any paper.

"He said, 'That would be the Soviet Union, plus White Russia, plus the Ukraine.' Then I said, 'By the way, if the conference in San Francisco should give you three votes in the Assembly—if you get three votes—I do not know what would happen if I don't put in a plea for three votes in the States.' And I said, 'I would make the plea for three votes and insist on it.'

"It is not really of any great importance. It is an investigatory body only. I told Stettinius to forget it. I am not awfully keen for three votes in the Assembly. It is the little fellow who needs the vote in the Assembly. This business about the number of votes in the Assembly does not make a great deal of difference."

A reporter asked, "They don't decide anything, do they?"

Roosevelt said, "No."

Then, he reminded his absorbed audience of three: "By the way, this is all off the record."

The President fiddled with some papers on a card table beside his chair. His 998th press conference was over. The three newsmen filed out, not knowing when next they would have the chance to pump the greatest news well they had ever known.

3

"We've Got Just Fifteen Minutes More"

A few minutes before noon on April 12th Bill Hassett strode into the Little White House, lugging the stuffed mail pouch that had finally arrived from Washington. Beside him walked Dewey Long, the solemn-faced White House transportation officer.

The President, sitting in his leather armchair, his back to the wall of windows that overlooked a broad valley of pines, was chatting with three lady guests. His two cousins, Misses Margaret Suckley and Laura Delano, each appeared to be in her forties. Miss Suckley had a sedate face, eyes hinting a private sadness, that occasionally would slip into a smile. She spoke in a soft monotone; her words were considered, sure. Miss Delano spoke faster; words less considered, less sure, but more forceful. Her nose and cheekbones were sharp; they seemed to come to points. Her face and quick manner were of a woman whose mind was thoroughly alive, whose busy world was almost under control, but which at any moment might get out of hand. Franklin

Roosevelt was fond of them both, especially their contrast when they were together. They were perfect companions on a vacation trip. They never burdened him with talk about affairs of state, but they seldom were silent for long, and never inattentive.

The third guest, Mrs. Winthrop Rutherfurd, an uncommonly attractive sandy-haired woman in her early fifties, inclined more to the art of listening. Mrs. Rutherfurd had become a friend of the Roosevelts in 1913 when thirty-one-year-old Franklin was Assistant Secretary of the Navy. Eleanor Roosevelt was sometimes overwhelmed by the combined problems of managing a family and meeting the social demands of official life in Washington. She tried getting along without a secretary but, as she later wrote, "found that it took me such endless hours to arrange my calling list, and answer and send invitations, that I finally engaged one three mornings a week."

Lucy Page Mercer, the twenty-two-year-old daughter of a Washington society matron who had fallen upon hard times, was suited by both training and need for the work. Eligible by background to become a friend of the Roosevelts as well as an employee, she soon became a friend. Within a few years she left their employ and married Winthrop Rutherfurd, a wealthy breeder of fox terriers, who was more than twice her age and whose family had long been socially intertwined with the Hyde Park Roosevelts. Rutherfurd died in 1944. His widow took up a life of near-seclusion in their lavish home at Aiken, South Carolina.

In 1943, Mrs. Rutherfurd had commissioned a portrait painter, Madame Elizabeth Shoumatoff, to paint a water color of the President. Now Roosevelt was returning the compliment. He arranged for Madame Shoumatoff to paint another portrait of him, which was to be given to Mrs. Rutherfurd's daughter. Madame Shoumatoff and

Mrs. Rutherfurd drove to Warm Springs together, arriving
Monday evening, April 9th. In their car they brought a
portrait photographer, Nicholas Robbins, to assist Madame
Shoumatoff. Many years later, Robbins was to say of the
Roosevelt family friend: "I have seen two smiles like that
in my life. One was on Leonardo da Vinci's 'Mona Lisa';
the other was Mrs. Rutherfurd's."

As Hassett greeted the ladies upon entering the room,
his sensitive eye registered the bad color and weariness of
Roosevelt's face. But the President seemed to be in good
spirits. To Dewey Long, whose eye was less sensitive to
subtle personal detail, the President looked no worse nor
better than usual.

The President was wearing a dark gray suit and a Harvard red four-in-hand tie. This struck Hassett as odd. Roosevelt was partial to blue bow ties. Even more odd, he was
wearing a vest. He disliked vests. Hassett assumed the Boss
was acceding to a request of the portrait painter. The
thought irritated him.

Hassett was never overly taken by Madame Shoumatoff's 1943 portrait of the President. He felt the artist
had made her subject too "pretty." She had done well, he
allowed, with the cape she posed him in, but he felt she
missed the soul of the man wearing it. Earlier in the week,
the artist had been mentioned in a conversation between
Hassett and the President.

"I will refer to her earlier picture," Hassett ventured,
"as one of the President *wearing a cape*, not as the President with a cape on."

Roosevelt, laughing, repeated the pun he thought he had
heard: "The President with a capon!"

Hassett said that that reminded him of the time William
Allen White called Herbert Hoover a "fat, timid capon."
Roosevelt, laughing again, said he hadn't heard that one.

Esthetics aside, Hassett was annoyed with Madame

Shoumatoff, because he felt she interrupted the President with too many measurements of his nose and requests to turn this way and that. He had meant, in fact, to talk with Dr. Bruenn about what he felt was "unnecessary hounding of a sick man." But despite Hassett's complaints against Madame Shoumatoff, Roosevelt seemed to be fond of her.

Because Hassett's load of mail was heavy, he suggested that perhaps the Boss might want to sign it after lunch. No, Roosevelt said, he would do it right away.

As Hassett sorted papers, Dewey Long sat beside the President. He reviewed plans for the President's trip to the San Francisco conference. He would leave Warm Springs on the 18th, arriving in Washington the next day, then depart via the B. & O. route to Chicago. Long proposed a choice of routes west of Chicago, pointing out one that would take the President through the Royal Gorge in Colorado. Roosevelt said he had already seen the Royal Gorge twice; he instructed Long to pick "the fastest way." It was the first time Long had ever known Roosevelt to show indifference to a routing and to set speed above a scenic adventure. Long folded his notes and left the cottage.

Hassett placed before the President a letter prepared for his signature by the State Department. Roosevelt read it closely. Then his face brightened. "A typical State Department letter," he said, looking pleased. "It says nothing at all."

Hassett put the signed letter on the chair that Long had vacated. Then he spread out a batch of diplomas for distinguished foreigners receiving the Legion of Merit; next a sheaf of postmaster appointments, including one for Panaca, Nevada. When they were signed, Hassett distributed them along the couch, on chairs, and around the floor. This was a method that Hassett had devised for coping with the inkiness of Roosevelt's signature. Blotting it

without smudging was almost hopeless. (Hassett's practice
has led to a legend that it is improper to blot a President's
signature; this, says Hassett, is untrue.)

They came to a bill just passed by Congress. It was
Senate Bill 298, which extended the life of the Commodity
Credit Corporation and increased the agency's borrowing
power. Roosevelt lifted his pen, looked up at his guests,
and said with schoolboy pride: "Here's where I make a
law."

Roosevelt wrote the word "Approved," and in a racy,
fragmented script added his name and the date.

From the entrance of the cottage there came a clatter-
ing. Madame Shoumatoff, tall, stately, and dark-haired, was
carrying an easel.

"Oh, come right ahead," the President called.

She set up the easel near the windows in the dining area
of the room. Hassett, pointing to the papers lying about,
apologized for the disarray.

The President said: "Bill is waiting for his laundry to
dry."

As Hassett prepared to go, Roosevelt said he would get
to the Allcorn barbecue at four-thirty, and that the other
staff members should go ahead at four as planned. At
seven, he would proceed to the minstrel show at Georgia
Hall. Then he remembered a message he wanted Hassett to
send to Frank Walker, the Postmaster General. He liked
Walker's idea that, upon arriving at San Francisco on April
25th, the President would buy the first sheet of postage
stamps commemorating the opening of the United Nations.
Hassett made a note of this final directive. Then he handed
the President a collection of documents to read as he posed
for the painter. One of these was a two-page report of
diplomatic developments that the State Department prepared each day for the President's personal attention. Hassett left.

Roosevelt gripped the arms of his leather armchair, lifted himself, and swung to a straight-backed Dutch-style chair that had been fitted with tiny rollers beneath its legs. It was a graceful, unnoticeable maneuver. (So unnoticeable that three days later at a press conference Madame Shoumatoff, describing the scene, said the President was seated in the leather chair when she began to paint.) He swung around to face the easel, which he could not have done in the leather chair. His right profile was lit by the sun from the long windows. His left profile was to Miss Suckley, who was sitting on the couch. Mrs. Rutherfurd was sitting to the President's right, her back to the windows.

Madame Shoumatoff placed a navy blue cape on Roosevelt's shoulders and meticulously arranged its folds. Then she stepped behind her easel.

The room grew quiet. The President began to read the papers before him.

Madame Shoumatoff sought certain typical, lively expressions on her subject's face which, because of his absorption in the papers, were now absent. She attempted to engage him in conversation. She said, in a cultured Russian accent, that she had recently seen the new stamp marking the centennial celebration of the State of Florida and asked if he had taken a hand in designing it.

He said, looking pleased: "I certainly did."

Joe Esperancilla, the houseboy, emerged from the kitchen with a tray of dishes and began to set the dining-room table for lunch. Arthur Prettyman, the valet, helped him. Daisy Bonner, the cook, followed them from the kitchen. She was carrying a round, dented, silver tray, and she placed it on the card table beside the President's chair. On it was a small cup of gruel, a creamer, a tiny sugar bowl, and a spoon. The cook had been instructed to bring him this snack before lunch each day as a weight-builder. The President, preoccupied, took a spoonful and left the rest untouched. Then he glanced at his watch. It was exactly one o'clock.

He said to Madame Shoumatoff: "We've got just fifteen minutes more."

The President became so absorbed in his reading that Madame Shoumatoff didn't dare ask him to look up. Because he had fallen out of his pose, she used her time for filling in colors.

"I noticed as his face would turn partly away from me," she was to say later, "that he looked younger than he had on the previous day. As I studied him he looked like a portrait done of him several years ago by Salisbury. . . . He looked strangely well."

Miss Suckley, sitting on the couch to the President's left, was crocheting. Miss Delano, stepping quietly about, was filling vases with flowers that she and Miss Suckley had picked that morning. Lizzie McDuffie, the maid, was passing through the entry, about to cross the front lawn to the guest cottage, where the beds of Madame Shoumatoff and Mrs. Rutherfurd needed to be made. Before leaving, Mrs. McDuffie turned to look into the living room. She noted that the President was sitting in the straight-backed chair with the tiny wheels and had a paper in his hand. She could also see Mrs. Rutherfurd facing him. He had just made a little joke and she was smiling.

"That is the last picture I have in my mind of Mr. Roosevelt," Mrs. McDuffie says. "The last I remember he was looking into the smiling face of a beautiful woman."

Several hundred yards away, Bill Hassett was just entering the dining room of Georgia Hall. More than a mile away, Grace Tully, Dorothy Brady, and Louise Hachmeister had finished their morning swim and left the pool. Dr. Bruenn, flat on his belly in the sun, too comfortable to go to lunch right away, had asked Hacky to reserve a sand-

wich and a bottle of milk for him at Georgia Hall. He'd
need some nourishment, he said, because he was to compete
in a golf tournament early that afternoon.

Miss Suckley, in the Little White House, continued her
crocheting. There was nothing she had found of great interest to read among the President's books in the wall of
shelves to her right: Elliot Paul's *I'll Hate Myself in the
Morning*, Owen Lattimore's *Solution in Asia*, a forbid-
ding treatise called *The Tropical Subsistence Homestead*,
O'Brien's anthology of *The Best Short Stories of 1915*,
the 1932 edition of *Who's Who in America*, Jacobson's
Progressive Relaxation, Earl Browder's *Teheran*, Helen
and George Papashvily's *Anything Can Happen*, *The Best
of Damon Runyon*, Douglass *The New Deal Comes to
Brown County*, and several dozen others. On the flyleaf of
each was the President's signature. He loved to spend a
relaxing evening signing books—even after a wearing day
of signing papers.

The President slid a cigarette into his holder and lit it.

In the stillness, Madame Shoumatoff, who had by now
given up all hope of winning the President's attention
from his papers, noticed that he raised his left hand to his
temple and pressed it. He slid the hand around to his
forehead and seemed to be squeezing it. Then his hand
flopped ungracefully down, as though fumbling for the
arm of his chair.

Miss Suckley's attention was caught by the gesture. She
thought he had dropped his cigarette in his lap and was
groping for it. At that moment, Miss Delano was stepping
out of the door of her bedroom behind the President. She
had just filled her vase.

Miss Suckley put down her crocheting and stepped over
to the left side of the President's chair. She asked: "Did
you drop something?"

The President pressed the palm of his left hand behind his neck. His head was leaning forward. His eyes were closed. He said very quietly: "I have a terrific headache."

He said it so quietly, no one heard it but Miss Suckley. It was inaudible even to Madame Shoumatoff about six feet away.

The President's arm slipped down and his head tilted slightly to the left. His body sagged between the thin wooden arms of the chair.

At that moment, the world, as it had been known for sixty-three years to the consciousness of Franklin Delano Roosevelt, tilted and spun and blurred out of focus.

The time was one-fifteen.

Miss Delano was now at his right shoulder. Each of the cousins grabbed a shoulder of his huge body to keep him from falling.

With aristocratic composure, Miss Suckley said to Madame Shoumatoff: "Ask the Secret Service man to call a doctor immediately."

The artist disappeared out the front door. Then Miss Suckley had a second thought. She lifted the phone next to the President's leather chair. In a momentary lapse of composure, Miss Suckley announced herself to the operator by a nickname which only intimates were permitted to call her.

"This is Daisy Suckley," she said. She instructed the operator to locate Dr. Bruenn and have him come immediately to the Little White House. She did not say why.

4

"I Knew It Was
the Last of Earth"

Outside the Little White House a Secret Service agent, Jim Beary, was relaxing in the growing warmth of the day. His repose ended when Madame Shoumatoff dashed from the cottage.

"Please call a doctor!" she said.

Beary disappeared through the kitchen door and phoned the cottage of another agent, Guy Spaman, who jumped into a car to fetch Dr. Bruenn at the pool.

But Bruenn was already hurriedly dressing. Louise Hachmeister had just called him on the poolside phone.

Hacky, on her way back from the pool, had stopped at her cottage to check her switchboard. When she rang the operator at the Foundation's central board, she learned that hardly a minute earlier Daisy had called—looking for Dr. Bruenn.

Daisy? Calling for Dr. Bruenn? Hacky, who assumed that only the cook would have called herself Daisy, said she would take over. She rang the Little White House kitchen.

"Daisy, who wants Dr. Bruenn?" Hacky asked. "Does the President want him for lunch?"

"Oh no, Miss Hacky," Daisy Bonner replied. "He's sick. The President is sick."

"All right, Daisy," Hacky said crisply. When she reached Bruenn, he told her to find George Fox, have him get Bruenn's bag from his cottage, and meet him at the Little White House immediately.

At that moment, Commander Fox, the Navy physiotherapist who gave the President a daily rubdown, had just left the dining room at Georgia Hall. He was enjoying a stroll in the sun in front of Hacky's cottage. She called to him from the window, repeating Bruenn's instructions. Fox disappeared down the road.

By the time Spaman's car arrived at the pool, Bruenn was dressed. As they sped the mile and a half to the Little White House, Bruenn tried to imagine what might have occurred. The President had been in fine spirits when Bruenn examined him at nine-thirty, just before his breakfast tray had come. His heart sounded fine. Although his blood pressure was high—180/110-20, an evidence of hypertension—it was not alarming; it had been running high for months. The President hadn't seemed tense. Often during Bruenn's morning visits, Roosevelt would bristle with cryptic barbs about the problems pressing his mind— lately, the post-Yalta behavior of the Russians. But there had been no such troubled remarks this morning.

The car skidded in the gravel driveway and Bruenn bolted into the cottage. The living-room door framed an awesome picture. Silhouetted against the windows, the bulky form of the President, his back toward Bruenn, was slumped in a soft heap. His head leaned loosely to his left. He was all alone, balanced and propped by the thin arms of the wooden chair. The cousins sat stiffly on the couch.

Bruenn ordered Fox and the houseboy, Joe, to help him carry the fallen man into the bedroom. They had trouble extricating his big, inert body from the tight arms of the chair. In the bedroom, they lowered the patient to his maple bed. Bruenn lifted his patient's shoulders to remove his coat.

The President stopped breathing.

Bruenn, astonished, released the shoulders, almost with a jar. The President started breathing again. It came loud, hoarse, almost like a snore. The patient's tongue had fallen back, obstructing the throat. There was a rigidity in the neck.

Bruenn had to get the patient's clothes off. He called for scissors. Fox dug a pair from the black bag. Fiercely, Bruenn sheared away at the President's clothes, tossing huge scraps to the floor.

Moments before, the pupils of the patient's eyes had been equal. Now the left one was dilating widely. The patient's pulse palpitated at 104. His blood pressure shot the indicator beyond its measured limit of 300.

The symptoms were all too clear. The President had suffered a cerebral hemorrhage; the only question was how serious.

To ease the surging blood pressure, Bruenn injected doses of aminophyllin and nitroglycerin into the President's arm. Then, with Fox's aid, he gently removed the remnants of the President's clothes and dressed him in pajamas with wide, pale blue stripes. Now Bruenn could only wait for new symptoms and treat them as they appeared; there was nothing else to do.

For the moment there was nothing anyone could do. Yet everyone felt a need to do something. Spaman drove back to the pool and brought his chief, Mike Reilly, to the cottage. Reilly phoned Bill Hassett and Grace Tully.

While members of the official family were rushing to the cottage, Madame Shoumatoff and Mrs. Rutherfurd, who were only visitors, were hastily preparing to leave. The artist phoned Nicholas Robbins, her photographic assistant, at the Warm Springs Hotel, telling him to pack his equipment quickly and bring her car to the guest cottage. Within minutes after the President had collapsed, the three visitors were gone from the grounds.

Daisy Bonner, who also felt the need to do something, raced to her friend, Lizzie McDuffie, who was making up Madame Shoumatoff's bed.

"Lizzie, why haven't you come over?"

Lizzie looked up. "Why? They're busy with their lunch over there."

"Didn't Arthur come and tell you what happened?"

"Why no, he didn't tell me anything happened."

Then Daisy said, almost whispering, "Oh, Lizzie—*I believe the President is dying.*"

"Why—why, Arthur, that dunce! Why didn't he tell me?"

Immediately, she was sorry she had said something so unkind about the President's valet. The two women raced to the President's cottage.

The people in the living room were silent; only occasionally, a whispered word. But from the bedroom, there came a slow dreadful series of long, deep, laborious, gravelly gasps.

These were the sounds that also greeted Hassett when, fearfully, he came into the house.

"The heavy breathing which I heard as soon as I entered the cottage told the story," Hassett was to write in his diary hours later. "I knew the President was mortally stricken. We sat in silence. Presently I went into the

President's bedroom. Dr. Bruenn and George Fox were with him. His eyes were closed—mouth open—the awful breathing. But the Greek nose and the noble forehead were grand as ever. I knew it was the last of earth. No one spoke. A little later, Grace Tully arrived. We spoke no word. Grace sat down, her lips moving in prayer. I did not return to the bedroom. It seemed to me that since Mrs. Roosevelt and Anna and the boys could not be at his bedside, we should leave him with the doctors. The awful breathing continued and convinced me that he was now beyond all earthly help."

At 2:05, Bruenn, having completed his emergency ministrations, called Admiral Ross McIntire in Washington. The President had been unconscious for fifty minutes. Bruenn reported the symptoms of the cerebral stroke and said there was partial paralysis and intense vasostriction. He said he would call again in five minutes.

McIntire put in a call to Atlanta for Dr. James E. Paullin, a distinguished internist and a former president of the American Medical Association. McIntire told Paullin to get to Warm Springs as rapidly as he could.

Then Laura Delano called Mrs. Roosevelt in Washington to tell her the President had fainted.

A half hour passed before Bruenn called McIntire again. He reported that the heart rate and breathing were better, color improved, and blood pressure showed signs of falling. But he said the condition was desperately serious.

Reilly dispatched a Secret Service car to patrol the main highway toward Atlanta in search of Paullin, to prevent state police from stopping him for speeding. But Paullin, a veteran of many wild night rides through the Georgia hills, was racing through short cuts along the back roads.

"I drove rapidly and expected to be picked up any moment," he recalled. "But I had decided to explain my

mission and ask officers to escort me to Warm Springs
without delay. I was not stopped, however, and never
slackened my speed. I arrived at Warm Springs at
3:28 P.M. . . ."

Dr. Paullin hurried into the Little White House. With a
curt nod he acknowledged the presence of those already
assembled in the living room. No word was spoken. He
marched directly to the bedroom door of the stricken
President. He had examined the President here before and
knew the house well.

In a report he later sent to Admiral McIntire, Dr.
Paullin described what he found:

"The President was *in extremis* when I reached him. He
was in a cold sweat, ashy gray, and breathing with difficulty. Numerous rhonchi in his chest. He was propped
up in bed. His pupils were dilated, and his hands slightly
cyanosed. Commander Bruenn had started artificial res-
piration. On examination his pulse was barely perceptible.
His heart sounds could be heard, but about three and a
half minutes after my arrival, they disappeared completely.
I gave him an intracardiac dose of adrenalin in the hope
that we might stimulate his heart to action. However, his
lungs were full of râles, both fine, medium and coarse, and
his blood pressure was not obtainable."

In the living room, each of the watchful, waiting group
was suspended in a world of private tensions. Each has told,
in interviews and in writing, what he remembers:

Mike Reilly: "It was a stricken and tense little crowd.
. . . Grace Tully sat quietly in a corner, frightened but
dry-eyed. Hassett was frightened and distraught. . . . I
don't know what Grace was thinking, but I never for a
single solitary second thought he'd die. I knew he was down,
but I knew he'd come up. I'd seen him in many a tough
spot before, and he'd yet to lose."

Lizzie McDuffie: "It was trying. *Lord,* it was trying.

They stood around and smoked. The ones who wanted to talk went way off from the house. All you could hear was the breathing. It was kind of like—*deep, steady, long gasps*."

Bill Hassett: "We spoke in whispers out on the terrace. I felt that the end was fast approaching."

Grace Tully: "Almost within seconds of Paullin's arrival, Bruenn was called again by Dr. McIntire. While on the phone he was summoned back. . . ."

Mike Reilly: "I heard Fox yell, 'Bruenn—Doc Bruenn —come here, quick.' Bruenn told Admiral Mac to hold on and hurried into the Boss's room. . . ."

Admiral McIntire (in Washington, hearing a clunk as Bruenn dropped his phone): "I heard him utter a startled exclamation, and the sudden silence made me know that he had been summoned back into the sickroom. It seemed ages that I waited, but it could only have been a matter of seconds. . . ."

Dr. Paullin: "There were no effects from the adrenalin except perhaps for two or three beats of the heart, which did not continue. Within five minutes after my entrance into the room, all evidence of life passed away. The time was 3:35 o'clock."

Bill Hassett: "The silencing of the dreadful breathing was a signal that the end had come, even before Dr. Bruenn emerged from the chamber of death."

Grace Tully: "In a minute or so, Bruenn was back. With a tragically expressive gesture of his hands he picked up the phone again."

Mike Reilly: "He said nothing. Just lowered his head and shook it. Then I knew I had been wrong and Doc and Bill had been right."

Grace Tully: "I knew what the message was before he spoke."

Bill Hassett: "Thus a good man met the solemn day

that awaits us all. Dr. Bruenn told Admiral McIntire that all was over."

Grace Tully: "My reaction of the moment was one of complete lack of emotion. It was as if my whole mind and sense of feeling had been swept away. The shock was unexpected and the actuality of the event was outside belief. Without a word or a glance toward the others present, I walked into the bedroom, leaned over and kissed the President lightly on the forehead. Then I walked out on the porch and stood wordless and tearless. In my heart were prayers and, finally, in my mind came thoughts, a flood of them drawn from seventeen years of acquaintance, close association and reverent admiration. Through them, one recurred constantly—that the Boss had always shunned emotionalism and that I must, for the immediate present at least, behave in this pattern. Bill Hassett, never more magnificent in his quiet dignity, took the phone after Bruenn to talk with Steve Early in Washington. Early's instructions were that no one should be told until he could reach Mrs. Roosevelt, at that very moment making a speech at the Sulgrave Club in Washington."

5

"The Amenities
Had to Be Observed"

Never in American history had a First Lady of the land
been so important and consistent a maker of news as
Eleanor Roosevelt; not merely social news—as on this
day, at the Sulgrave Club—but political news as well. Un-
becoming as it seemed to traditionalists, Mrs. Roosevelt
spent much of her time in such un-First-Lady-like activities as giving, of all things, *speeches;* about such un-First-
Lady-like subjects as the rights of labor, equality for
Negroes, economic opportunities for youth, and the problems of the United Nations. Often she took daring po-
sitions on these questions—even more daring than her
husband had taken. Critics of the President called her a
radical busybody; supporters of the President believed she
was his most useful instrument for sounding out what the
people were thinking.

Her mail was enormous for a First Lady. She believed
that ordinary people who write their feelings to a President's wife express themselves more frankly than those

who write to a President. She read her mail carefully, always sorting out those letters she thought were especially revealing of popular thought. She would bring small piles of these letters to show her husband at their private dinners or on any of the rare occasions when their affairs permitted them to have a quiet hour together. She believed that a President, to be a great national leader, had to carry on a constant "dialogue" with the people.

And she took part in a considerable national dialogue of her own. Mrs. Roosevelt was the author of a daily column syndicated in hundreds of newspapers. She made extensive speaking tours, using even these as sounding boards by engaging in question-and-answer periods.

Many people say of Mrs. Roosevelt that she is a homely woman, but that as soon as she starts to speak she appears wondrously beautiful. Her voice is not pretty; it seems almost artificially high-pitched and unsure. But when she speaks, she glows with utter good will.

She is almost impossible to anger. When she lands a verbal thrust at an opponent—a maneuver at which she is skilled—her sentence ends with the kindliest softening of her face and a disarming double twinkle of her eyelids. She makes it appear that her victim, down deep where it counts, is loved.

An instrument in Mrs. Roosevelt's dialogue with America was—most extraordinary for a First Lady—the regularly scheduled press conference; not about social matters if she could help it, but *political* matters. One such press conference was scheduled at 11 A.M. on Thursday, April 12th, as her first appointment of the day.

Mrs. Roosevelt told the lady reporters who gathered in her sitting room at the White House that she would be leaving in a couple of days for speaking engagements in New York. The big plan in her future was to accompany her husband to San Francisco for the opening of the

United Nations conference. The reporters asked what she would do at the conference and what she expected the United States and the Soviet Union to do about governing a conquered Germany. Mrs. Roosevelt's eyelids began to flutter. Her slow-warming smile played across her face as she parried the questions, trying to explain that the proper authorities would undoubtedly make those decisions when the time came. But there was a tone in the questions that challenged her. Then, in gracefully turned high-pitched vowels and deliberate consonants, she spoke her piece:

"We must accustom ourselves to remember we are one of three nations with a responsibility of waging war, and once there is a United Nations organization, countries once occupied have a right to express their opinion too.

"We will have to get over the habit of saying what we as a single nation will do. When we say 'we' on international questions in the future, we will mean all the people who have an interest in the question. A United Nations organization is for the very purpose of making it possible that all the world's opinion will have a clearing place.

"It will supply every nation with a free expression of the people. Until then our State and War Departments know more than we do, and carry the responsibility. The matter should be fully in their hands."

When the ladies of the press left, Mrs. Roosevelt received a series of callers. At three o'clock—it was two o'clock at Warm Springs, and the President had been unconscious for three-quarters of an hour—Charles Taussig, an advisor to the United States delegation to the San Francisco conference, arrived. Shortly after they began to talk, Mrs. Roosevelt was given a signal by her secretary, Malvina Thompson, of an important telephone call. Laura Delano was calling from Warm Springs.

Miss Delano told Mrs. Roosevelt that the President had

fainted. Mrs. Roosevelt asked terse questions, calculated to elicit all Miss Delano could tell her, yet to reveal almost nothing to Mrs. Roosevelt's guest. She might have been talking, for all anyone could tell, to her daughter, Anna, about the condition of her grandson Johnny's infected throat.

Mrs. Roosevelt hung up and began to conclude her conference with Mr. Taussig. But again Miss Thompson signaled her. Admiral McIntire was calling. Gracefully but rapidly, Mrs. Roosevelt ended the conference and picked up the phone.

McIntire reported his call from Dr. Bruenn. He said he was not alarmed, but suggested that Mrs. Roosevelt prepare to leave with him later in the day for Warm Springs. He had ordered a Navy plane. Mrs. Roosevelt asked if he thought she should cancel a speaking engagement she had in half an hour. No, advised McIntire, a cancellation followed by an unexpected trip to Warm Springs might cause great comment. She said she would keep the engagement.

In a black White House limousine, Mrs. Roosevelt left for the Sulgrave Club to attend the seventeenth Annual Tea and Entertainment of the Thrift Shop, one of Washington's fashionable charities. She arrived promptly at her appointed hour, four o'clock.

The Annual Tea of the Thrift Shop was a function that Mrs. Roosevelt had not missed for years. She took her seat at the head table in the Sulgrave Club between Mrs. John Allan Dougherty, chairman of the event, and Mrs. Woodrow Wilson. A society reporter at a nearby table described her as "looking unusually smart and in soaring spirits."

Each of the invited ladies had brought a "white elephant" to be sold at the Thrift Shop, a store to which used articles of value were donated for resale. The proceeds were used to support six charity organizations for children.

Mrs. Dougherty introduced Mrs. Roosevelt for a short talk, and the First Lady paid high tribute to Mrs. John R. Williams, one of the moving spirits of the Thrift Shop who was absent because of illness.

After Mrs. Roosevelt's talk, Miss Meredith Howard took over as master of ceremonies. She introduced Chago Rodrigo, a Latin-American troubadour. Then Miss Howard brought on the highlight of the entertainment, Helena Bliss and Lawrence Brooks, the stars of *Song of Norway*, playing on Broadway. They were followed by Evalyn Tyner, a pianist.

A few seconds after Miss Tyner began to play—the time was now 4:50—Miss Howard tiptoed behind the head table and whispered to Mrs. Roosevelt that she was wanted on the telephone. One of the ladies nearby was later to say that the message gave Mrs. Roosevelt "a quick start, obvious only to the persons immediately around her." She quietly left the table.

Mrs. Roosevelt describes the moment: "Steve Early, very much upset, asked me to come home at once. I did not even ask why. I knew down in my heart that something dreadful had happened. Nevertheless the amenities had to be observed, so I went back to the party. . . ."

Mrs. Roosevelt waited until Miss Tyner's piano piece was finished, helped applaud her, and then rose to say: "Now I'm called back to the White House and I want to apologize for leaving before this delightful concert is finished."

The women gave her an ovation as she swept out of the room escorted by Mrs. Dougherty.

"I got into the car and sat with clenched hands all the way to the White House," Mrs. Roosevelt has said. "In my heart I knew what had happened, but one does not actually formulate these terrible thoughts until they are spoken."

During the tension of the ride, Mrs. Roosevelt perhaps permitted herself to weigh the meaning of some odd things she had recently observed. She was soon to write:

"On the first of March he addressed the Congress, and I knew when he consented to do this sitting down that he had accepted a certain degree of invalidism. I found him less and less willing to see people for any length of time, wanting and needing a rest in the middle of the day. He was anxious to get away and I was pleased when he decided to go to Warm Springs. . . . He invited his cousins. . . . I knew that they would not bother him as I should have by discussing questions of state; he would be allowed to get a real rest and yet would have companionship—and that was what I felt he most needed.

"For the first time I was beginning to realize that he could no longer bear to have a real discussion, such as we had always had. This was impressed on me one night when we were discussing with Harry Hooker the question of compulsory military service for all young men as a peace-time measure. Harry Hooker had long believed in this and had worked for it. I disliked the idea thoroughly and argued against it heatedly, probably because I felt Harry was so much in favor of it that Franklin seemed to be getting only one side of the picture. In the end, I evidently made Franklin feel I was really arguing against him and I suddenly realized he was upset. I stopped at once, but afterwards Harry Hooker took me to task and said I must not do that to Franklin again. I knew only too well that in discussing the issue I had forgotten that Franklin was no longer the calm and imperturbable person who, in the past, had always goaded me on to vehement arguments when questions of policy came up. It was just another indication of the change which we were all so unwilling to acknowledge."

Arriving at the White House at last, Mrs. Roosevelt went directly to her sitting room on the second floor. She instructed Malvina Thompson to inform Steve Early she had arrived.

Early was later to tell newsmen: "When she came back, Admiral McIntire and I went to her sitting room and told her the President had slipped away. She was silent for a minute and her first words were: 'I am more sorry for the people of this country and of the world than I am for ourselves.' "

Those words, as reported by Early, were to be quoted in the next twenty-four hours by nearly every newspaper in America and most others around the world. People were to quote them in the streets. Editorials were to be written about them. A few people felt that the saying was evidence of a lack of emotion on the part of Mrs. Roosevelt about personal matters. But most people felt otherwise. One newspaper columnist wrote a searching, speculative piece on what she meant by it. He said the sentence was an example of Mrs. Roosevelt's accurate understanding, even under the pressure of personal shock, of F.D.R.'s position as a leader of the world, which transcended his position as head of a family.

The odd fact is that Mrs. Roosevelt is certain she never made the statement at all. The words were called to her attention by admirers very shortly after she was supposed to have spoken them—and even then, when the details of the agonizing drama were fresh to her memory, the words had the sound of utter newness to her.

So perhaps they were merely words that Steve Early, an experienced and imaginative newsman and public relations expert, wished she had said. Or perhaps they repre-

sented a thought born in his mind with such poetic force
that he thought he heard them spoken.

After Steve Early had informed her of the news, Mrs.
Roosevelt composed a telegram to be sent to her four
sons, each in some distant place on war duty. Then she
said that she wanted to prepare immediately to go to
Warm Springs. She suggested that Early send at once for
the Vice-President of the United States.

6

"I'll Be on
All the Networks"

At eleven o'clock in the morning of Thursday, April 12, 1945 (while the President, many miles away, was reading his newspaper in bed and thinking seriously about getting up), the Majority Leader of the United States Senate, Alben W. Barkley of Kentucky, swiveled high on the Senate dais which, by provision of the Constitution, was the official perch of the Vice-President of the United States. He surveyed the array of ninety-six desks curved before him, which almost without exception were unoccupied, and he banged down a gavel.

The Vice-President, Harry S. Truman of Missouri, who knew that nothing of great moment was expected to take place in the early minutes of the Senate session, was elsewhere in the hidden convolutions of the Capitol building, taking his sweet time.

The handful of Senators in the chamber rose and lowered their heads, as the Reverend John Falconer Fraser, D.D., Pastor of the National Baptist Memorial Church of Washington, spoke an appropriate prayer:

"O Thou who art above all governments, eternal in Thy majesty and higher than all principalities and powers . . . we would ask Thy blessing of the President of the United States and all who are related to him in the affairs of Government.

". . . We thank Thee for the promise of victory so near, victory in a war we are compelled to fight because it is the only road to peace. . . . Now we come asking Thy special blessing, O Lord our God, upon the thousands of homes receiving sad messages from abroad. Give the consolation and the comfort and the ministry of Thy divine spirit in every house of mourning. . . . This we ask in and through that name that is above every name. Amen."

The chair recognized Senator Raymond Willis of Indiana, who, with evident feeling and no reticence in putting the mother tongue through extensive exercise, requested the unanimous consent of the Senate to have inserted in the *Congressional Record* an article from the New York *Times* which pointed out that America's ally, Russia, for mysterious and possibly sinister reasons, was sending an inordinate number of diplomats to Cuba.

During Senator Willis' speech, Vice-President Truman strolled into the chamber. He climbed to the dais, twinkled his eyes merrily through thick eyeglasses that had a way of making his eyes look surprisingly big, shook hands with his good friend, Senator Barkley, and replaced him in the chair. He grinned a few greetings around the chamber.

The Vice-President handed a few official communications to the reading clerk, who announced them to the Senate. There was a letter from the Secretary of the Treasury containing the annual report of the Exchange Stabilization Fund; a resolution by the Senate of Pennsylvania announcing a welcome home celebration after the war for General George S. Patton, to which the President of the United States was invited; a request from the Alaska legislature to do something about preserving reindeer in the national parks of Alaska, specifically by removing all restrictions upon the killing of wolves and coyotes, the natural enemies of reindeer; and a resolution from the Saturday Lunch Club of Minneapolis commending the President for his efforts to further the cause of peace and unity.

Senator Albert Hawkes of New Jersey rose to present a petition by the Sons of Italy in America asking that Italy be invited to the San Francisco conference. The Vice-President then recognized Senator Scott Lucas of Illinois. Senator Lucas reported that the Committee to Audit and Control Contingent Expenses of the Senate had approved the continuation of a fund voted by the Senate on July 1, 1943, "for the purposes stated in said resolution." Before Senator Lucas could sit down, Senator Kenneth Wherry of Nebraska was on his feet, asking Senator Lucas to explain what "said resolution" had said. Lucas didn't quite know; he turned to Senator Tom Connally of Texas. Senator Connally said the fund was to pay for the lunches of distinguished foreigners so that Senators wouldn't have to pay for them out of their personal resources. Since the money was not all spent, the Committee thought the surplus ought to be carried over into the present session. Senator Wherry, still suspicious, asked how much money was left. Senator Connally didn't know, but thought that perhaps Senator Lucas did. Senator Lucas didn't know. Then Senator Connally said he thought the surplus was only two or three hundred dollars. Senator Wherry sat down.

Other Senators introduced bills and resolutions. During this procedure, Vice-President Truman left his chair and walked out of the chamber. He returned in about two minutes.

Senator William Langer of North Dakota arose to suggest the absence of a quorum. This action made it necessary for the clerk to call the names of each of the ninety-six Senators. Throughout the Senate wing of the Capitol, an insistent bell vibrated. The clerk began to recite each name in a slow deliberate drone, pausing after each name to mark with ceremonious slowness the presence or absence of each Senator. Senators were suddenly pouring through the doors, forming into chatty groups, answering "Here!" when their names were called. The roll call provided a respite from their legislative labors, which was perhaps what Senator Langer had in mind when he called for it. When all was done, fifty-two Senators had answered the muster. A quorum was present. The world's greatest deliberative body could continue its work.

Senator Dennis Chavez of New Mexico caught the Vice-President's eye and was given the floor. "Mr. President, I should like to make a parliamentary inquiry of the chair."

Mr. Truman said, "The Senator will state it."

"The Committee on Education and Labor was in session this morning when the quorum call came. The Chairman of the Committee asked us to be back in committee in fifteen minutes. . . . Is it necessary to ask for official permission to leave the chamber now in order that we may go back to the Committee?"

"If the Committee is meeting in the Capitol building," Mr. Truman replied, "and the members are immediately available on call of the Senate, there is no reason for asking permission."

"What if it is meeting in the Senate office building?"

"Then," said Mr. Truman decisively, "they must ask permission, because some time is required to get from the Senate office building to the Capitol."

"Mr. President," Senator Chavez announced, "I ask for permission to leave the chamber."

Senator Kenneth McKellar, the President pro tempore of the Senate, who would permanently assume the chair if for any reason the Vice-President were to vacate his office, lifted his aging bones to a standing position.

"Mr. President," he said, "I am under an engagement to make a Jefferson Day address at Knoxville, Tennessee, tomorrow night and I ask unanimous consent to be excused until next Monday."

Senator Sheridan Downey of California was on his feet. "Mr. President, will the Senator yield?"

Senator McKellar turned to Downey, puzzled. A few Senatorial heads turned. "I yield."

"Reserving the right to object, does the distinguished Senator intend to make the usual eloquent and oratorical address he generally makes?"

A titter flowed through the chamber and galleries. The Senator from Tennessee was too surprised to make an eloquent and oratorical reply: "I am unable to say."

"I'm sure he will do so," said the Senator from California, "and therefore I make no objection to his being absent."

Mr. Truman granted the leave. Then he recognized Senator Connally again, this time in his capacity as the Chairman of the Foreign Relations Committee, to begin the debate on the main business before the Senate, the ratification of a water treaty with Mexico. As the Senator warmed to his subject, Mr. Truman left the chamber again.

He returned in time to hear an extended speech by Senator Ernest McFarland of Arizona, pleading for ratification of the treaty. The Vice-President listened with considerable interest. Then Senator Alexander Wiley of Wisconsin asked for recognition. He began to approach his subject, backed off, waltzed gracefully around to another entrance, and approached it again.

"Mr. President, I feel somewhat hesitant," he began, "to

speak on the subject of the treaty now before the Senate. I was a member of the Committee which for more than four weeks considered the treaty. I saw partisans of Texas, of California, and perhaps one or two other states take charge of the sessions by main force. . . . We are at a period in our own history when international politics engage the attention and the thought of our people. The thinkers and statesmen of all nations are likewise engaged. International politics cannot be separated from what we call international economics. The prosperity of every nation depends upon the economic set-up of the nation. Economics, of course, is dependent upon consumption, production and distribution. Because the nations of the world have grown closer together . . ."

There was no getting away from the fact that being the Vice-President of the United States could be enormously dull. Senators, seeking escape, had a place to go. Their desks were piled high with mail from constituents, their reception rooms cluttered with visiting delegations representing potential voters, their committee meetings alive with engaging debate and diverting wit. Harry S. Truman of Missouri had had a taste of such activity and had savored it. While he was a Senator, he'd had more fun than at any time in his life.

During the war years, Senator Truman had enjoyed the sweet headiness of reading his name in headlines almost every day. Perhaps not many Americans could correctly recite the name of the committee of which he was chairman, the Special Committee to Investigate the National Defense Program. But a good many had heard of it by its informal name, the Truman Committee. It was an important, crusading, aggressive, watchdog committee that sought out neglect and corruption in the vital parts of the country's war machine: the metals industry, rubber, shipbuilding, aircraft, labor relations, defense housing, army camp construction. At one point, Washington newspaper-men voted Senator Truman as the civilian who knew most about the war effort aside from the President himself. This was indeed something for a Missouri farm boy whose formal education had not stretched beyond high school.

He was not among the Senate's florid orators. His sentences were always short, his words simple. When he got the floor, he could seldom think of anything to say except the main point that he had stood up to make. He'd make it and sit down. But despite these limitations, the Senators respected and admired him. He was loyal to his party and his friends, and he showed courage. Courage is an attribute that is not universal on the floor of the Senate; but there, as anywhere else, it is universally admired.

So in 1944, when the Democratic Party was split over a battle between Vice-Presidential candidates, it was natural that certain party peacemakers began to eye Senator Truman as a possible happy medium. The people knew his name, even if he had not been blessed with a magnetic personality. He was identified with a positive, hard-hitting crusade, yet nobody owned up to disliking him. The liberal wing of the party was confident that President Roosevelt wanted the renomination of Henry A. Wallace. The conservatives, however, would have no more of Wallace's visions of "the century of the common man"—they rallied, instead, around the candidacy of James F. Byrnes of South Carolina, former Senator, former Supreme Court Justice, and then Director of Economic Stabilization. Truman promised to nominate Byrnes. Finally Roosevelt, who seemed to many of his lieutenants not to care very much who was to become his Vice-Presidential candidate, in the last minute gave a penciled note to Robert E. Hannegan, National Chairman of the party, authorizing the approval of Truman. The New York *Times* called Truman "the second Missouri Compromise."

Two days after Truman became Vice-President, Roosevelt left for Yalta. In all, of the eighty-two days since the new term had begun, the President had been in Washington for less than a month. Except for Cabinet meetings, Truman had had only two known appointments with Roosevelt, on March 8th and March 19th. If Roosevelt was planning to make Truman a working part of his administrative machinery, he had made no serious move to do so as yet. So Truman and his wife, Bess, did what Vice-Presidents and their wives traditionally do. They went to parties and dinners. He sat dutifully on the dais of the Senate, giving Senators permission to go make their speeches elsewhere, and sometimes he ran across the hall to his office to greet and inspire a group of awe-struck tourists.

This is not to say that the Vice-Presidency did not offer its lofty and significant moments. Just two days earlier, on April 10th, the Senate was closing its debate on an extension of the Lend-Lease Act, the heart of Roosevelt's program for supporting America's allies with ships and war matériel. Since the war was almost over, the Republicans moved to put on the brakes. Senator Robert A. Taft of Ohio introduced an amendment prohibiting the President from using the Lend-Lease program for postwar relief and rehabilitation in other lands. The amendment was favored by thirty-four Republicans, four Democrats, and one Progressive (Robert La Follette, Jr., of Wisconsin); it was opposed by thirty-seven Democrats and two Republicans. When the clerk handed his tally sheet to the Vice-President, Truman stood up, grinned triumphantly, and announced: "The vote is thirty-nine to thirty-nine. The chair votes 'No.' "

It was an important victory for Franklin D. Roosevelt.

But that was two days ago. Now Senator Wiley was talking interminably on a subject that had little glamour and even less promise of the excitement of a tie vote. The

Vice-President leaned over his elevated desk and whispered to a clerk at the desk below that he would like a sheet of plain white paper. He took a fountain pen from his pocket, struck a busy pose, and began to write:

Dear Mamma & Mary: I am trying to write you a letter today from the desk of the President of the Senate while a windy Senator . . . is making a speech on a subject with which he is in no way familiar. The Jr. Sen. from Arizona made a speech on the subject, and he knew what he was talking about. . . .

We are considering the Mexican Treaty on water in the Colorado River and the Rio Grande. It is of vital importance to Southwestern U.S. and northern Mexico. Hope we get it over some day soon.

The Senators from California and one from Utah and a very disagreeable one from Nevada (McCarran) are fighting the ratification. I have to sit up here and make parliamentary rulings—some of which are common sense and some of which are not.

Hope you are having a nice spell of weather. We've had a week of beautiful weather but it is raining and misting today. I don't think it's going to last long. Hope not for I must fly to Providence, R.I., Sunday morning.

Turn on your radio tomorrow night at 9:30 your time, and you'll hear Harry make a Jefferson Day address to the nation. I think I'll be on all the networks, so it ought not to be hard to get me. It will be followed by the President, whom I'll introduce.

Hope you are both well and stay that way.
Love to you both.
Write when you can.

At long last, Senator Wiley surrendered the floor. Senator Barkley moved for a recess until noon the following day. The time was 4:56.

It was a good time, the Vice-President decided, to pay a

call on the distinguished Speaker of the House of Representatives. Speaker Sam Rayburn just about now would
be leaving his office by a private door and furtively entering a little known chamber down the hall, which his
predecessors had come to call the "board of education." A
little known drawer in a little known desk of this room
contained an abundant store of miniature bottles of good
bourbon spirits. In the colorful phrasing of the few hearties
ever permitted access to the room, a sip of good fellow-
ship there was called "striking a blow for liberty." This
was the pleasant ritual that attracted Harry S. Truman as
he made his way through the corridors of the Capitol.

The mood of the building, the hurried steps of busy men
tapping along the timeless, dark marble floors, was as it
always was. Truman strolled from the Senate wing into
the center hall. A familiar tranquillity hung high in the air
above, in the great dome among the lazy rays of a declin-
ing sun. There was no hint in the air, in the tap of foot-
steps, on the earnest faces, that twenty-one minutes earlier,
he, Harry S. Truman of Missouri, had ascended to the office of President of the United States.

The "board of education," already assembled, was composed on this day of Lew Deschler, Parliamentarian of the
House of Representatives, and James M. Barnes, a White
House legislative assistant, as well as Speaker Rayburn.
Augmented now by the distinguished new arrival, the
group made good company. They were weathered masters
of the specialized science of putting votes together—direct-
ing dissimilar men to move simultaneously in the same
direction. It is a technical art, as distinguished from the cre-
ative art of dreaming political visions, and most of its prac-
titioners proudly feel they have their feet on the ground.

Sam Rayburn was just handing Harry Truman a freshly
poured glass of bourbon and tap water when he remem-

bered that a few minutes before, a call had come to his
office for Mr. Truman, transferred there from the Vice-
President's office. Casually, the Speaker passed on the message that Steve Early had called from the White House and
that he wanted Mr. Truman to return the call right away.
As Mr. Truman recalls Early's voice, it was strained.
Early said merely: "Please come right over and come in
through the main Pennsylvania Avenue entrance."

Truman turned to Rayburn and said apologetically that
he was wanted at the White House, but that he would be
back shortly. Then he added that he didn't know what was
up, so the summons ought not to be mentioned to anyone.

The recollections of the next few moments are strangely
conflicting. Newsmen have quoted Mr. Truman's three
companions as saying that his face turned pale. A clerk in
the Vice-President's office was quoted as saying Mr. Truman dashed in looking greatly agitated, grabbed his hat,
and made a single, terse utterance that would qualify as the
understatement of the century: "I'm going to the White
House."

According to Mr. Truman's version, he was not upset
at all:

"I did not know why I had been called. . . . The President, I thought, must have returned to Washington for the
funeral of his friend, Bishop Atwood, the former Episcopal Bishop of Arizona, and I imagined that he wanted me
to go over some matters with him before his return to
Warm Springs.

"On previous occasions when the President had called
me to the White House for private talks he had asked me
to keep the visits confidential. At such times I had used the
east entrance to the White House, and in this way the
meetings were kept off the official caller list. Now, however, I told Tom Harty, my government chauffeur, to
drive me to the main entrance."

Truman's black limousine drove through the northwest gate at 5:25 and swung halfway around the long semicircle drive to the front entrance of the White House. Mr. Truman was ushered to an elevator and then to Mrs. Roosevelt's second-floor study. The moment he entered the room, he knew that something uncommon was in the air. He couldn't quite tell why. Mrs. Roosevelt seemed calm and, as always, dignified. Steve Early's face was deep red, but it was always deep red. Perhaps the strangeness was the presence of the Roosevelt daughter, Anna, and her husband, Colonel John Boettiger.

Mrs. Roosevelt stepped forward and placed a gentle arm on Mr. Truman's shoulder. "Harry," she said quietly, "the President is dead."

"For a moment," Mr. Truman recalls, "I could not bring myself to speak. The last news we had had from Warm Springs was that Mr. Roosevelt was recuperating nicely. In fact, he was apparently doing so well that no member of his family, and not even his personal physician, was with him. All this flashed through my mind before I found my voice."

When he found it, he said: "Is there anything I can do for you?"

Mr. Truman has never forgotten Mrs. Roosevelt's reply:

"Is there anything *we* can do for *you?* You are the one in trouble now."

Mr. Truman was again speechless. The overwhelming fact that faced him was hard to grasp.

"I had been afraid for many weeks that something might happen to this great leader," he recalls, "but now that the worst had happened I was unprepared for it. I did not allow myself to think about it after I became Vice-President. . . . It seems to me that for a few minutes we stood silent, and then there was a knock on the study door."

The man at the door was Edward R. Stettinius. As Secretary of State, he was keeper of the Great Seal of the United States and charged with ascertaining and proclaiming the passing of a President. Everyone in the room was struck by his odd appearance. The Secretary of State, who was regarded as one of the handsomest men in the government and was certainly one of the most suave, was standing there crying.

Mr. Truman snapped suddenly into a posture of briskness. He asked Steve Early and Secretary Stettinius to summon the members of the Cabinet to a meeting as quickly as possible. That was his first order as the unsworn Chief Executive of the United States. Then he turned to Mrs. Roosevelt and asked what she planned to do. She said she wanted to go to Warm Springs at once. Then she asked if it would be proper for her to travel in a government plane.

Without hesitation, Mr. Truman made his second decision as the nation's leader. It would be perfectly right and proper, he said, and a grateful nation would insist on it.

Mr. Truman turned to Early and they took whispered inventory of certain arrangements that had to be made. Among them, they had to arrange for Mr. Truman to place his hand on a Bible and swear to execute faithfully the duties of his new office. Then he left the room, descended to the first floor, and walked under a covered terrace to the West Wing. He approached an oval room, a room that was one of the most inaccessible of all rooms in the United States: the office of the President.

7

"Is the War Over?"

While Mrs. Roosevelt, in her sitting room at the White House, was tensely awaiting the arrival of Harry S. Truman, guests were beginning to arrive at the barbecue party planned for her husband at Warm Springs.

A festive greeting had been prepared for him as a surprise. There was to be country fiddle music, something the President loved. Ruth Stevens had persuaded Bun Wright, a seventy-five-year-old hill character who could saw the frolicking phrases of a mountain square-dance tune into slices of pure joy, to tote his fiddle up to Pine Mountain. And Mr. Wright had brought two friends, Reuben Bridges to play guitar, and Leonard Williams from down the road at Chipley, Georgia, to play second fiddle.

When they began to play, Ruth Stevens breathed a sigh; at last the party was on. One early arrival was Ray Hoover, the Western Union man in charge of lines to the Little White House; others were Ed Clement and Lewis Asbell of the Southern Bell Telephone Company, who made sure official calls kept going smoothly; and Don Fischer of the National Broadcasting Company, who had arrived in Warm Springs only an hour before to handle Friday night's Jefferson Day address by the President for all the networks.

Now Mrs. Stevens looked around for members of the President's staff, who were expected at four, a half hour ahead of the President. None had yet appeared.

At 4:10, however, Major DeWitt Greer, the head of the Army Signal Corps unit, showed up. As he made the rounds of celebrants, he observed that their spirits were warming fast, aided by glasses of old-fashioneds. After greeting them, he checked the short wave units his men had set up in Frank Allcorn's barn.

Bun Wright struck up "She'll Be Comin' Round the Mountain," a warm up for the President's arrival. This was the tune he had played for Mr. Roosevelt at the housewarming of the Little White House in 1932, when he matter-of-factly announced that he, Bun Wright, was the best breakdown fiddler in the country. Mr. Roosevelt had readily agreed.

One night soon after that housewarming, Mr. Roosevelt visited Bun Wright and his neighbors in a poverty-stricken, isolated mountain hollow, called the Cove. Wright did a clog dance that night for the President, then began ripping tune after tune from the strings of his fiddle. He modulated from one to the next, calling out, "Mr. Roosevelt, giving you 'Cackling Pullet.'" When that was about played out, he called, "Now give you 'Fiddler's Dram.'" And then, "Now giving you a little bit of 'Devil's Dream.'" The people of the Cove, who are favored by few visitors from the world outside, later said that this great man from the government had been sent by God to see them. Roosevelt, interested as always in natural resource projects, had talked to them about damming up the stream that ran through the Cove, so the people could have themselves a lake to swim and fish in. But the people told him sadly that the stream was too muddy, that they'd get nothing but a muddy lake. Roosevelt never did build the dam.

At about 4:20, Merriman Smith began to feel irritated because none of the White House staff had arrived. Every inch the party lover, he wanted everyone to be settled and happy—and properly launched by the old-fashioneds—before the President got there. He asked Major Greer to check on what was holding up the staff.

Greer went to the radio in the barn, returned, and told Smith: "I don't understand the double talk I'm getting."

Greer surmised that one of the staff was being delayed by a call from Washington and the others were waiting for him. Smith excused himself and went to the barn. Signal Corps Sergeant Wayne Shell was sitting beside his short-wave portable, reading a Western magazine.

"Wayne," said Smith, "how about letting me call the Little White House to see if the Boss is on the way?"

The Sergeant picked up a hand microphone and, with professional nasality, honked into it: "Indiana to Pine— Indiana to Pine—come in please."

"Pine to Indiana—Pine to Indiana go ahead."

"Is there any sign of movement?"

"No—no sign of movement."

Smith, no fanatical respecter of Army prerogatives, took the mike from Shell's hands.

"Pine—who is this please?"

"This is Anderson." Anderson was a Secret Service agent. "Who is this?"

"This is Smitty, Andy. What the hell is going on down there?"

"Smitty, I honestly don't know. There just isn't anything doing."

"The President is supposed to be here in a few minutes."

"Yeah, I know. But there's nothing moving yet. Want me to give you a call?"

"No, Andy, I'll get on the phone and talk to Hacky."

Smith returned to the cottage, exasperated. He asked Allcorn's pretty daughter, Janet, to show him the phone. It was an old-fashioned, coffee-grinder set. He cranked for the operator and gave her the number of the Foundation switchboard. When he got it, he said acidly: "Ring the White House board."

Hacky's voice came in. "Yes, please."

"Hacky, this is Smitty. Why aren't you people on the way? What's holding things up?"

Hacky said she didn't know. That is, she'd find out in a minute. She'd find out and call back as soon as she could. Before he could speak, Hacky clicked off. She didn't sound like herself at all.

Seconds later, the Allcorn phone rang. It was Hacky— for Smitty.

"Smitty?" she shouted. The imperturbable operator was unmistakably in a panic. "Mr. Hassett wants to see you. Get the other two boys and go to his cottage as fast as you can."

"Hacky, what the hell is going on?"

"Smitty, I can't say any more. Just get down here as fast as you can."

"Is the war over?"

"I don't know what he wants to talk to you about."

Harold Oliver of A.P. and Bob Nixon of I.N.S. were talking together in the driveway. Smith cut over to them and quietly said, "Come with me."

Major Greer, a few feet away, read Smith's face and came over. "What's up?"

"Can you take us down to Hassett's cottage right away? Something awful big is going on."

They climbed into Greer's big, fast Lincoln convertible, calling to the others that they had to take care of something and they'd be right back. The car sped down the winding, narrow mountain road, skidding at each twist.

"The ride took about five minutes," Harold Oliver recalls. "It was tense. We knew something pretty big must be up. But there wasn't much said. Just a couple of remarks speculating that it could be a collapse in Europe. My mind was occupied trying to figure out the mechanics of how to transmit whatever the news was. It was going to be urgent and would have to move fast."

Merriman Smith: "The first thing I thought of was a major break in the war. Maybe Hitler died. I'm sure nobody thought Roosevelt might be dead. Anybody says he did, well, he's just . . ."

Bob Nixon: "I knew that either the war in Germany was over or Roosevelt was dead. I could tell by the sound in the air. A newsbreak is like an exploding shell. When I was in England, we'd hear those German shells coming over from Calais. We could tell by the whistling sound before it burst what kind of shell it was. Experience tells you."

Smith: "I was first one through the door. Hassett was standing near the fireplace of his living room, his face gray."

Nixon: "Running up the steps and across a screened-in porch, I saw Grace Tully through an open window. She was on the couch, crying."

Miss Tully: "From the expressions on our faces they probably knew what the announcement was to be. . . ."

Smith: "When I saw Grace Tully's tear-swollen eyes, I knew she was not crying about the end of the war. I remembered there were four telephones in Hassett's cottage. And one was only about two feet away from me—on the radiator in his living room."

Oliver: "Smith grabbed a phone a couple of feet behind Hassett. Nixon and I had to dive for phones in each of two adjoining bedrooms."

Smith: "Hassett cleared his throat and fiddled with two or three small pieces of paper in his hands."

Hassett: "They had no inkling of what was coming—their air that of slight resentment because their revel had been interrupted. I told them to get paper and pencil. They did so leisurely and indifferently."

Nixon: "At a moment like that, time becomes lost. You build up such a head of steam inside yourself, that everything stretches out. Split seconds become hours."

Smith: "Hassett stepped away from the fireplace. . . . I picked up the telephone."

Miss Tully: "Hassett was standing near the center of the living room. 'Gentlemen,' he said quietly, 'it is my sad duty to inform you that the President of the United States is dead. He died at 3:35 o'clock this afternoon, Central Standard Time.'"

Smith: "When I heard him say 'Gentlemen, it is my sad duty . . .' something in my head went 'boom!' I knew what it was."

Hassett: "After I made a brief statement of the time and cause of death, I suggested that they get their flashes and bulletins off, as I had asked Dr. Bruenn to come down and give them the medical statement to round out the story."

Oliver: "On the phone, Hacky said, 'Just a moment.' It seemed like an hour. I think she wanted to get us each a line and turn us on simultaneously."

Smith: "Hassett said Steve Early was announcing the story simultaneously in Washington. We didn't want the Washington boys to reach our offices first."

Nixon: "All of a sudden I could hear my long-distance operator in Atlanta yacking with an operator in Asheville, trying to get the call routed. I yelled for her to cut out the foolishness and get me Washington. This was Priority One—an urgent White House call."

While they waited, the reporters shouted questions at Hassett from their phones.

"What was the cause of death?"

"A massive cerebral hemorrhage."

"Had you seen the President today, Bill?"

"Yes, at about noon. He signed some bills and some mail."

"Was he ill then or in good spirits?"

"He seemed fine. He joked about all the 'laundry' I had to dry."

"Who was with him when he was stricken?"

He replied that an artist was sketching his portrait. Hassett believes that he mentioned Madame Shoumatoff by name. The name that was to appear in early dispatches from Warm Springs, however, was "N. Robbins," the name of Madame Shoumatoff's photographer.

Smith: "I heard telephone switchboards yanked apart, and then—it seemed hours, but it was only a few seconds —I heard the most welcome voice I ever heard in my life . . . our operator in Washington. . . ."

Major Greer, still standing by his car outside, had hardly had time to shut off his motor. The words of Hassett and the reporters pierced the afternoon stillness, and he couldn't help but hear it all.

He slumped into the front seat, numbed. Then, as in a daze, he drove away.

His car skidded to a halt in Frank Allcorn's red clay driveway. A few of the guests noticed that Greer had returned alone. The reporters had not come back. But only a few noticed; the rest kept laughing and the fiddlers went on with their tune.

Greer waved his hands at the fiddlers. To Ruth Stevens, he said, "Stevie, stop the music."

The fiddles faded sourly into a terrible silence. Everyone turned to Greer.

Greer put his arm on Allcorn's shoulder. "Frank," he said—but he wasn't speaking to Frank. He seemed to be addressing everybody. "I guess we won't be able to have the party."

His voice was strangely shrill. He said: "The Boss is dead."

Ruth looked at him incredulously, seized her face with spread, taut fingers. Major Greer took her shoulders, lowered his head, and began to shake with childlike sobs.

Bun Wright, his wizened face fixed in naked bewilderment, slowly lowered his fiddle and pulled off his battered hat. After a while, he began to say, very quietly, over and over, "What a good man to leave us. What a good man. . . ."

8

"Flash—F.D.R. Dead"

Late in the afternoon of Thursday, April 12th, Arthur F. Hermann, a writer for International News Service, left the White House press room and was strolling up 14th Street, N.W., in Washington after what could hardly be described as a hard day at the office. Unknown to the nation at large, the President was away from Washington. White House news was sparse; also it was dull.

Hermann turned a corner and entered the Times-Herald Building, went upstairs to the I.N.S. bureau, and headed for his desk to grind out a few items of small significance. Someone was using his typewriter. "Sit still," Hermann said, and he set to work at an available machine at the main news desk. A dozen employees—news editors, reporters, and three dictation girls—were scattered about. Hermann scanned a news handout from the Reconstruction Finance Corporation and began to tap out a story.

On the desk he had appropriated, there was a telephone key box with a row of tiny lights and switches. At exactly

5:45 P.M., one of the lights blinked for attention. Hermann ignored it; the light would show on other key boxes at other desks.

Nearby, Betsy Tupman, a dictation typist in her late teens, was reading a paper-bound novel of a type she called "chiller dillers." She flicked a switch and said into her phone, "I.N.S."

A male voice said with noticeable urgency: "Give me Mr. Slater quick. This is the White House calling."

J. Harold Slater, the managing editor, had gone home at 4 P.M. Betsy called to Erwin D. Sias, the day news editor: "Line thirty-three quick. The White House is calling."

Hermann's head turned. Just a short while earlier he had been told at the White House that the lid was on for the day. That meant that reporters could return to their offices assured that no more routine news would be released. In the event of an important newsbreak, the three major news services would be informed simultaneously through a conference telephone call. He noted that the light on his box—for line thirty-three—was a trunk line. It struck him as odd that the call had not come over the direct line which the bureau, at considerable expense, maintained to the White House. Then he remembered that Louise Hachmeister, the unerring chief of the White House switchboard, was away with the President's party. A less experienced hand was obviously at work. Hermann wondered if this could be a conference call—which would probably mean a story of first-page merit.

Sias, a man of many preoccupations, instead of picking up his phone, motioned to Hermann to take it. At the same time, Arthur Hachten, the night managing editor, sitting at a desk next to Hermann's, picked up his extension. Betsy put down her book, adjusted her earpiece, and prepared to type whatever she was to hear.

A few blocks away, in the National Press Building, a petite, dark-haired dictation girl, Ann Fischer, was sitting at the switchboard of the United Press. The regular operator, Romilda Flanagan, had gone home at five. Two men sat at the day desk, Julius Frandsen, the bureau manager, whose face was always pinched with quiet suffering; and Joseph L. Myler, a tall, beefy rewrite man. Their day was almost done and the pace had grown lazy. A teletype operator, Jerry Eldridge, was sneezing his head off from a bad case of spring hay-fever. He was seeking escape from his infirmity by reading, through teary eyes, the text coming in by teletype from New York, a column of amusing comment by Frederick C. Othman. Such non-urgent material always moved at the end of the day, after the flow of pressing news dwindled.

At 5:45, Ann Fischer's switchboard buzzed.

"United Press," she sang lightly. She listened a moment, turned her head, and called "Desk." This meant a news item.

Joe Myler lifted his phone.

"This is the White House," a voice said. "Hang on."

Myler knew the lid was on; this must be a conference call. He thought of switching the call to a dictation girl; let her wait for the announcement and type it out. But none of the girls was free. Myler leaned back and waited.

At the Associated Press, in the Washington Star Building at 11th and Pennsylvania, Gardner L. Bridge was sitting at what A.P. men call the "general desk" when the call came. His boss, W. L. Beale, Jr., was nearby. Bill Todd, a teletype operator, dawdled at his machine, waiting to go home. Bridge, recognizing that a conference call was being organized, signaled a dictation girl to listen with him and type the announcement.

At all three offices, the collection of telephone listeners

heard a click, and a woman's voice said: "Hang on." Soon, the voice said it again: "Hang on." Then a male voice began to call a roll. He called I.N.S. first. Hermann answered, "I.N.S. here." Then A.P. Bridge said, "Here." Finally, U.P. Myler said, "Here." Then the voice said, "Just a moment, please." About two minutes had gone by since the calls had first come.

Then the phones clicked again and a new male voice —it sounded faint—said: "This is Steve Early." He was talking fast.

At I.N.S., Betsy Tupman typed "Steve Early." At U.P., Myler, pencil in hand, scribbled "Steve Early."

". . . I have a flash for you."

Betsy typed "Flash." Myler scribbled "-flash."

". . . The President died suddenly this afternoon at . . ."

At I.N.S., Hermann, firing a glance at Betsy to make sure she was taking dictation, slammed down his phone. He was on his feet, his stunned mind grasping for a hard, quick phrase. Art Hachten, at the next phone, whispered in disbelief, "F.D.R. *dead?*"

Hermann, converting Hachten's shocked question to a statement, bellowed like an infantry sergeant: "Flash! F.D.R. Dead!"

Charles Sparkenbaugh, the night wire operator, reared back and stared at Hermann. Then he heaved his body forward. He pressed four times on his bell key, then typed:

FLASH
      WASHN—FDR DEAD.

Sparkenbaugh glanced at the office electric clock. Its hand was between 5:47 and 5:48. He typed:

INS WASHN 4/12/547PPH36.

Milt Eglin, punching the same flash on the day wire, looked at the clock the same second and timed his message 5:48.

The text of the I.N.S. flash was the shortest in the history of news transmission.

Hermann ran to the teletype machines to make sure the flash was right. Then he ripped a strip of paper from Betsy's typewriter—while Early was still talking and she was still typing—and began to dictate from the first words of Early's statement.

In the next office, William K. Hutchinson, the roaring, quick-tempered I.N.S. bureau chief, heard the most electrifying word that is ever spoken in a newspaper office: "Flash!" He leaped from his desk, glared at the teletype machine, and demanded of Hermann: "How do you know?"

Hermann said: "I recognized Early's voice."

Hutchinson bounded back to his desk. He had dropped his phone in the middle of a conversation with William Theis in the Senate Press Gallery. Into the phone, he shouted an order. To the others who heard it, the command was so surprising, it sounded for the moment like something far-fetched—indeed, irrelevant. He roared at Theis: "Roosevelt's dead! *Go find Harry Truman!*"

At United Press, Joe Myler, straining to hear Early's faint, fast speech, scrawled:

> Steve Early—flash
> Prest died this aftern
> at

Then a girl's voice broke in. The girl, dumfounded, cut off the White House spokesman with an utterly understandable interruption: "Do you mean President *Roosevelt?*"

Early, exasperated, snapped back: "Christ! There's only one President. *Of course* I mean President Roosevelt."

Then Early completed his first sentence: ". . . at Warm Springs, Georgia."

Myler seized the moment of interruption to motion wildly to Julius Frandsen and fiercely whisper the flash. Frandsen leaped to Myler's desk, stared at the eight scrawled words, and froze. His face turned red, then paled. Myler jerked his thumb insistently toward the teletype like a desperate hitchhiker.

Frandsen asked, almost hissing: "Are you sure it's Steve?"

Myler nodded emphatically. Frandsen straightened up and roared at Jerry Eldridge, the sneezing teletype operator:

"FLASH. WASHINGTON. PRESIDENT ROOSEVELT DIED THIS AFTERNOON."

Eldridge timed his flash at 5:48.

Myler, meanwhile, was taking down Early's words in big scribbles. His second sheet read:

> at Warm Springs, Ga.
> deth resulted from
> cerebal hemorrhage
> —V-P Truman has been
> notified. Called to
> W hse & informed By
> Mrs. R.

He handed the sheet to Frandsen, who started dictating to Eldridge. On a new sheet, Myler kept scrawling:

> Secy of State has been
> advised. Cab meeting

> has been called. 4
> boys in service have
> been sent message by
> their mother which
> sed—(no quote)

On another sheet, he continued:

> that the president slipped
> away this afternoon.
> he did his job to the
> end as he wud
> want you to do.
> Bless you all and
> all our love. Mrs.
> R. signed the
> message "mother."

Myler wasn't quite sure if Early had said "slipped away" or "slept away." But he continued scribbling on a new sheet:

> Mrs. R., Adm. McIntyre
> & Steve Early will
> leave WA by air t aft
> for warm Springs.

Another sheet:

> We expect (Steve talking)
> to leave Warm S tmro
> a.m. by train for
> Wa. funeral
> services will be
> held Sat. aft.
> east room of W hse.

Frandsen was still grabbing the sheets and dictating. On a fresh one, Myler wrote:

> Interment will be
> at Hyde Park Sunday
> aft. ~~Detailed~~
> No detailed aranns or
> exact times have
> been decided on
> as yet.

On a final sheet, Myler wrote:

> for details hv get
> from man at
> Warm Springs.

Myler said, "Thank you, Steve." The others chimed in, and the call was over.

At the Associated Press, Gardner Bridge ripped the flash from a dictation girl's typewriter and shoved it at his boss, Bill Beale. As seconds slipped past them into history, Bridge and Beale conducted a hasty conference to decide whether to dateline the flash "Washington" or "Warm Springs." They settled on Washington. Then Beale turned to Bill Todd, the teletype man, and delivered what amounted to a short talk:

"FLASH—WASHINGTON—PRESIDENT ROOSEVELT DIED SUDDENLY THIS AFTERNOON AT WARM SPRINGS, GA."

The A.P. flash was timed at 5:49.

In the frantic race among the wire services for transmission of a flash, the largest of them, A.P., had lost at least a full minute to the smallest, I.N.S.

Within two or three minutes after the flashes were dispatched, each of the offices received a call from its excited reporter at Carver Cottage in Warm Springs.

Diagonally across the street from the National Press Building at 14th and New York Avenue, a young news editor named David Brinkley of radio station WRC was marking yellow sheets of news copy, when he heard the I.N.S. teletype ring four times. It was not loud; but it was the most arresting sound he knew. It meant a flash—rapid news of the highest order of importance. He dashed to the machine.

The two words he read were staggering.

He tore the words from the teletype and brought them to Leonard Schleider, the news manager. Brinkley heard himself giving his boss a command: "Wait till we get confirmation from another wire."

Brinkley remembered the day when the A.P. machine rang a flash from London of the Allies opening a western front. It later turned out to be a phony report. The trans-Atlantic line had been open, and someone in London punched out the item as a prank.

Less than a minute later, the U.P. machine rang twelve times—the U.P. signal for a flash.

Then Brinkley and Schleider remembered that their station was at that moment hooked up to the N.B.C. network. The program on the air was *Front Page Farrell*, a newspaper adventure serial for children. They decided to wait. The network would break into the program to bring the flash to all America. . . .

At 485 Madison Avenue, New York, the headquarters of the Columbia Broadcasting System, *Wilderness Road*, a serial for children based on the life of Daniel Boone, was on the air. In the news room, John Charles Daly pored

Franklin D. Roosevelt Library

President Roosevelt's alarming physical decline during his final days is apparent in this photograph, taken on March 24, 1945, less than three weeks before his death. It was the last picture taken of him in the White House.

Franklin D. Roosevelt Library

Unusual personal devotion characterized the relationships between Roosevelt and members of his official family. A close aide, with the title of Secretary to the President, was William D. Hassett, with whom he was photographed *(above)* on April 9, 1940. At the President's famous trinket-cluttered desk *(below)*, he was photographed on March 4, 1943, with Grace Tully, his private secretary; Stephen Early, press secretary; and Major General Edwin "Pa" Watson, appointment secretary.

Franklin D. Roosevelt Library

Before the President's death was announced to the world, members of the Cabinet were summoned to the White House. Secretary of Labor Frances Perkins, arriving at the Cabinet Room, shares her grief and fear with an associate. Attorney General Francis Biddle *(left)* and Secretary of Agriculture Claude Wickard are awaiting the entrance of the Vice-President.

Franklin D. Roosevelt Library

Wide World Photos

The swearing-in of Harry S. Truman was delayed until 7:08 P.M., while the assembled officials waited for the arrival of his wife and daughter. The ceremony was later re-enacted to accommodate newspaper photographers. At 7:12 the new President was still posing.

President Roosevelt collapsed while posing for this water-color portrait by Madame Elizabeth Shoumatoff. Two hours and twenty minutes later, he was dead.

© 1945, Franklin D. Roosevelt Warm Springs Memorial Commission

Franklin D. Roosevelt Library

Next morning a crowd gathered at the Warm Springs station to witness the President's farewell. A railroad car that had served as his traveling office, the *Conneaut,* was stripped of all furnishings except a wall mirror. In this car, he was carried on the mournful journey to Washington.

Wide World Photos

Franklin D. Roosevelt Library

The President's body was drawn through the streets of Washington...

Franklin D. Roosevelt Library

Wide World Photos

...as

500,000

of

his

countrymen

came

to

say

good-bye.

Franklin D. Roosevelt Library

Franklin D. Roosevelt Library

Franklin D. Roosevelt Library

At the Roosevelt ancestral estate in Hyde Park, the President was taken up the climbing, winding "river road..."

Franklin D. Roosevelt Library

Franklin D. Roosevelt Library

and then, led by a young crucifer and the aging Reverend Angus Dun,...

Franklin D. Roosevelt Library

the President's widow, flanked by his daughter Anna and son Elliott, walked behind the casket as servicemen carried it to the grave.

over late items in preparation for his 6:15 national newscast. At about thirty seconds past 5:47, four bells clanged from the I.N.S. teletype.

Lee Otis, the assistant news editor, leaped to the machine and read:

FLASH
WASHN—FDR DEAD.

He shoved the yellow strip at Daly. Daly's first urge was to run for a mike. But he, too, waited for another machine to confirm the news. As he waited, he realized he did not want the confirmation to come. He did not want to put it on the air. Franklin D. Roosevelt was his friend. Then the U.P. bells rang. . . .

Daly bounded into the main news studio. He waved to Harry Higgs, the engineer, and drew his finger across his throat, meaning "Cut! Give me the network." In a few seconds his microphone was open to the nation. Daly extemporized:

"We interrupt this program to bring you a special bulletin from C.B.S. World News. A press association has just announced that President Roosevelt is dead. All that has been received is just that bare announcement. There are no further details as yet, but C.B.S. World News will return to the air in just a few moments with more information as it is received in our New York headquarters. We return you now to our regularly scheduled program. . . ."

At 5:49:25, N.B.C. broke into *Front Page Farrell* with the announcement. Seconds later, the news shattered the progress of *Captain Midnight* on A.B.C. and *Tom Mix* on Mutual.

The evening sun was bringing an orange tranquillity to the Hudson River Valley. Master Sergeant Newell E.

Fisher, a cornet player in the Army band at West Point, New York, lolled in a camp chair behind the band quarters. With him were his wife, Ethel, and another couple. His two children, eight-year-old Barbara and six-year-old Newell, Jr., were contributing to Fisher's peace of mind by staying out of sight. They were in the house listening to a children's program on the radio.

Newell, Jr., appeared at the door and called: "Mommy, you know what it said on the radio? It said the man in the light house is dead."

"All right, Junior," Mrs. Fisher replied absent-mindedly. She assumed the child was relating an episode on the program.

Then Junior's sister was at the door.

"Oh *no*, Ma, Junior's got it wrong," Barbara called. "It said the man in the *White* House is dead."

Sergeant Fisher and his wife and their two friends looked at each other in the strangest way. Then, without a word, they went into the house.

9

"He Was Just
Like a Daddy to Me"

Vida Jane Butler, clinging to a leather strap near the front of a crowded streetcar in Washington, D.C., was thinking pleasant, private thoughts. She was almost twenty-two, and very pretty, with a turned-up nose and earnest brown eyes. Vida Jane was a wartime "government girl."

An old beau from back home in Memphis was in town. He was clever and handsome, and he was a date. In wartime Washington, that was something in itself.

The streets outside were alive with government workers going home. The streetcar stopped and a garish woman climbed in. Her hair was dyed red; her dress was black, loose, and out of style. Her rouge and powder were moist. The woman deposited her coin and, holding her hand in mid-air, stared into the crowd of passengers. Her face was limp, doughy, helpless.

"Listen," she said to anybody—to everybody. "President Roosevelt died." Her voice lifted to a higher, shriller pitch and she said it again: "President Roosevelt died."

The world paused. Vida Jane watched and felt nothing. All was still. Until a Negro man sitting in front of her murmured, ever so low: "Oh, my God."

Vida Jane pushed her way out of the streetcar. She had to find out. As she stepped to the curb, two girls from her office grabbed her, one by each arm. Their eyes were frightfully wide.

"*Did you hear?*" one of them said. "*The President died.*"

A few blocks away, another government girl was crossing the lobby of the fashionable Mayflower Hotel on the way to her room upstairs. It was not a hotel where government girls ordinarily lived, but Lela Stiles was no ordinary government girl. She worked in the White House, analyzing mail and digesting editorial opinion for the President himself. She had just come from the beauty parlor, getting her hair fixed for Friday's Jefferson Day Dinner, when she almost collided with Anis Azer, the counselor of the Egyptian Legation. Seizing her arm, Azer asked: "Where did you just come from?"

"If you can't tell that, I've wasted my money," Miss Stiles replied. "From the beauty parlor."

"No, no. I mean before that. When did you leave the White House?"

"About four o'clock."

"Call the White House. At once, please."

He pulled her toward a row of phone booths, pressing a coin into her hands.

"But why? What's all the mystery?"

"Nothing, nothing at all. Just a whisper between two men in the lobby as I passed. Please call."

Miss Stiles, bewildered, recited a number to the operator. She heard clicking, chatter, confusion. Then the operator said, "In view of what has happened, we cannot get through. The President has just died."

Miss Stiles turned slowly to Azer, staring. She put back the receiver. She said nothing.

"That was the whisper I heard," Azer said, "but I would not believe it. This is the most dreadful thing that ever happened to the world."

Several blocks away, at the British embassy, a small group of attachés were chatting with a reporter from the Associated Press when a telephone rang. The man who answered it bolted upright in his chair. Then he slowly lowered the phone. He repeated to the others what he had been told. For fully ten seconds, no words were spoken. Then one of the men said, "My God." Another said, "He hasn't looked at all well lately." And a third said, "It's the beastly changeable weather." The man who had taken the call said, as though to himself, "I wonder what it will mean—to the war."

At the Sulgrave Club, the annual entertainment for the Thrift Shop had just ended. The ladies gathered in the dining room for tea. They chatted in small, jolly groups. A few speculated on the reason for Mrs. Roosevelt's departure. They hoped it meant that some word of peace had been received. Then, like a crack of lightning, the news flashed across the room. The women stood hushed. One looked around quickly for Mrs. Woodrow Wilson; the shock to her would be awful. But the elderly lady had already gone.

Across Pennsylvania Avenue from the White House, a silent crowd was gathering in Lafayette Square. People were coming from all directions. They just stood there and looked at the white-columned mansion. Occasionally a woman sobbed. Men removed their hats. Hardly anyone turned to go away.

The corridors of the Capitol building were gloomy, almost empty. Both houses of Congress had long ago re-

cessed. A reporter, stalking the halls for someone—anyone
—who might say something about the incredible news,
saw a tall, stooping, weary figure standing alone by a
window. He was a young Representative from Texas,
Lyndon B. Johnson, one of the hundred or so recently
obscure men who came to be called Roosevelt's "Young
Guard." The reporter didn't ask him anything. But Representative Johnson began to talk—quietly, privately.

"I was in the Speaker's office when it came. The phone
rang and the Speaker answered. He didn't say anything at
all that I could hear—just a kind of gulp. Then he hung
up and looked at me. Finally, he said the President was
dead.

"I was just looking up at a cartoon on the wall—a cartoon showing the President with that cigarette holder and
his jaw stuck out like it always was. He had his head
cocked back, you know. . . .

"He was just like a daddy to me always. He was the one
person I ever knew—anywhere—who was never afraid.
. . . I don't know that I'd have ever come to Congress if
it hadn't been for him. But I do know I got my first great
desire for public office because of him—and so did thousands of young men all over the country. . . .

"The people who are going to be crushed by this are
the little guys—the little guy down in my district, say,
who makes $21.50 a week driving a truck and he has a
decent house to live in now, cheap, because of Mr. Roosevelt.

"God—God, how he could take it for us all."

In another North American capital—at Ottawa, Canada
—a news teletype outside the press gallery of the House of
Commons rang the insistent bells of a flash. A reporter put
down his pencil and hurried out. He tore a strip from the
newsprinter and stopped in his tracks. Then he ran to the

gallery. The yellow strip was passed from hand to hand
by reporters, without a word. Then one of them took it
down to the Chamber.

Prime Minister Mackenzie King was away from the
House. Debate was being led by the Right Honorable
C. D. Howe, the American-born Minister of Reconstruc-
tion and Supply. The slip passed silently down a row of
House members and was handed to Mr. Howe.

He stared at the yellow scrap of paper as though unable
to believe his eyes. The House, sensing something extraordinary, hushed. Mr. Howe announced the death of the
President of the United States. The floor and visitors galleries sat stunned. The leader of each of Canada's four
parties stood up to say what words of grief he could find.
The House adjourned.

In New York City, the news poured and spread like a
scalding fluid into the streets, into office-building lobbies
and restaurants and theaters and bars, through subway
trains jammed with rush-hour crowds. People who heard
the news in the street raced into the caverns of the subway
saying to total strangers, "Did you hear the news? President Roosevelt died." The agony swept through the trains.
Passengers hearing it, elbowed their way out, bumping
against those coming down the stairs, to seek confirmation
in the streets. They didn't have to ask. Everywhere the
electrifying words: "Did you hear the news? Roosevelt
died."

Housewives left dinners on stoves and clustered in front
of shops. Shopkeepers faced radios toward the streets and
turned them up loud. The alarm center of the New York
Fire Department sounded "four fives" to all firehouses—
the dreaded signal that a fireman had died on duty.

At Times Square, policemen on horseback fought to
keep crowds on the sidewalk so cars could get through.

The electric bulbs that girdled the Times building to flash the latest news had been darkened for the war. But people kept looking up at the dead bulbs. A man shouted, "Where are those damned newspapers?"

On Lenox Avenue in Harlem, a Negro man said to a small crowd, "Don't worry. He was a great man with great ideas. He didn't let any grass grow under his feet. His plans are made and somebody's gonna carry them out." On Rivington Street on the Lower East Side, someone asked a Jewish housewife if she'd heard the radio. "For what do I need a radio?" the woman cried out. "It's on everybody's face."

In the lobby of a Park Avenue hotel, the whispered word burned the ears of the wife of a prominent Wall Street lawyer. She entered an elevator, clenching a glove, impatient to get to a radio. Half-a-dozen passengers crowded the little car. Behind her, a man's voice broke the silence. "So he's finally dead. Isn't it about time?" The woman turned around slowly, eyes wide. Then, in a most uncharacteristic gesture, she lashed her glove across the man's cheek. The door opened and she stepped out.

In the village of Hyde Park, alongside the Hudson River, the bells of St. James Episcopal Church began to peal. Its senior warden, Franklin D. Roosevelt, occupant of the third pew on the left side of the aisle, had departed this life.

At Groton School in Groton, Massachusetts, 185 students and their teachers were just sitting down to supper. Someone darted into the dining room and whispered into the ear of the Headmaster, the Reverend John Crocker. He rose. He looked pale. The babble of boys' voices tapered to a respectful silence. The Reverend Mr. Crocker announced that the President, a member of the class of

1900, had just died. Leaving his plate untouched, he led the boys to a nearby schoolroom. There the assembly prayed.

At that moment, to the west, tornadoes were tearing up the state of Oklahoma. Sixty-eight citizens were dead or about to die under collapsing buildings. In the town of Muskogee, while black winds whistled, the Associated Press teletype in the office of the Muskogee *Phoenix* rang out a flash. The editor, torn between a private urge to run for his life and a professional urge to record the destruction of his neighbors' lives, ran to read the flash—which he assumed was a report of the storm. He read. He blinked. He read again. It was too much to understand. *Roosevelt? Dead?* The wind outside was whistling the end of the world. *At this moment?* The machine began to rap out a more detailed, explanatory bulletin. Outside, there was a mighty crash. The machine stopped. The power lines were out. The machine would tell him no more.

Still further west, in a garage at 5000 South Broadway, Los Angeles, a forty-two-year old mechanic, George Hughey, was working on the engine of an automobile, when a fellow worker brought him the news. Hughey put down his tools and shuffled to the garage door, as though to think it over with the benefit of a breath of air. He said he felt terrible; so did everyone else. Then he said, "I hurt all over." Hughey walked back to the car he had been repairing. He fell against its fender. A few minutes later, in an ambulance on the way to the Georgia Street Receiving Hospital, Hughey died.

In a muddy town called Dulag on Leyte Island in the Philippines, where it was then early morning, Colonel James Roosevelt of the United States Marine Corps, intelligence officer of Amphibious Group Thirteen, Pacific

Fleet, was lying on his cot. In a few minutes, he would go fetch breakfast.

At the door, an orderly appeared. He fidgeted, then said, "I have something for you, sir." The orderly dropped a piece of paper on the cot and ran out. It was an official bulletin to the fleet announcing the death of the Commander in Chief. A few minutes later, a personal radiogram arrived for Colonel Roosevelt. It said: "DARLINGS: PA SLEPT AWAY THIS AFTERNOON. HE DID HIS JOB TO THE END AS HE WOULD WANT YOU TO DO. BLESS YOU. ALL OUR LOVE. MOTHER."

Young Roosevelt sat alone, too numb to think of anything very clearly. But he remembers thinking: *Pa is a casualty of the war, just as if he had been stopped by an enemy bullet.*

The magic of short-wave radio, which pierces the invisible walls separating warring nations, carried the flash into the heart of Tokyo. An announcer for Radio Tokyo repeated the bulletin to his people and said, to the puzzlement of American monitors: "We now introduce a few minutes of special music in honor of the passing of this great man." But the music did not last long. Japan's new Premier, Kantaro Suzuki, who had heard the news, rushed to the radio studio and went on the air himself. Befuddling American eavesdroppers even more, he said: "I must admit that Roosevelt's leadership has been very effective and has been responsible for the Americans' advantageous position today. For that reason I can easily understand the great loss his passing means to the American people and my profound sympathy goes to them."

In Chungking, China, Generalissimo Chiang Kai-shek, an early riser, had started his day's work at dawn. Shortly before six A.M.—when it was approaching six P.M. in

Washington and New York—he was sitting alone at break-fast. An aide raced in with the short-wave bulletin. For a moment, the Generalissimo sat stunned. Then he left his plate and retreated to meditate.

Westward still, across the vast reaches of Asia and Europe, it was a few minutes before midnight in London. Prime Minister Winston Churchill was entering his study at No. 10 Downing Street to read a few hours' accumulation of news reports. He had just returned from a large dinner party for British and Commonwealth delegates who were about to depart for the San Francisco conference. It had been a long day. In an outer room a telephone rang; an aide answered. The caller said he was from the United Press, and read a terse flash that had just been received. The aide said, "Good Lord!" He hurried to the Prime Minister's door, knocked impatiently, and turned the glass knob. Churchill was standing by his desk, papers in hand. "Sir," the secretary quavered, "President Roosevelt died a short time ago."

Churchill was later to write, "I felt as if I had been struck a physical blow." He sat down, wordless and motionless for a full five minutes. Then in a voice utterly tired and lonely he said, "Get me the Palace." Churchill told the news to the King's private secretary, Sir Alan Lascelles, who immediately brought it to the King. After many minutes, Churchill lifted a pen and addressed a radiogram to Mrs. Roosevelt: "I FEEL SO DEEPLY FOR YOU ALL. AS FOR ME, I HAVE LOST A DEAR AND CHERISHED FRIENDSHIP WHICH WAS FORGED IN THE FIRE OF WAR. I TRUST YOU MAY FIND CONSOLATION IN THE GLORY OF HIS NAME AND THE MAGNITUDE OF HIS WORK." He signed it simply "CHURCHILL."

At the moment the flash reached the United Press bureau in London and was telephoned to Churchill, it was

also received in the newsroom of the B.B.C. The time was
eleven minutes before midnight. A news broadcast was
scheduled for midnight. Nothing disturbs the meticulous
scheduling of the B.B.C., so for eleven minutes the news
waited. In an extraordinary gesture, however, a B.B.C.
employee telephoned the Rainbow Club, a large canteen
for American servicemen in London's West End, and politely suggested that the canteen turn on the midnight news
broadcast for an announcement of uncommon importance.

The advance warning was repeated at the Club and the
radio was turned on at full volume. In one corner, a ping-
pong game continued. The cafeteria line kept shuffling.
The battle-hardened young men could take important
news or leave it. At exactly midnight, the somber voice of
B.B.C. announcer Frederick Allen said: "It is with deep
regret that we report the death of Franklin D. Roosevelt.
He died suddenly this afternoon. . . ."

The ping-pong game stopped. Trays rattled as men set
down their food. *"What did he say?"* *"Did you hear the
same thing I did?"* An American radio correspondent,
Douglas Edwards, bolted out of his chair and charged into
the street. Frederick Allen's voice was still intoning the
announcement: "It was the President who, in the grim
days of Dunkerque, shipped rifles and vital supplies to
Great Britain to ward off what he had already seen as a
danger to the United States. . . ."

Two men carried a blackboard from the basement and
one of them chalked two not-quite-correct sentences:
"President Roosevelt died noon. Truman sworn in as President." The word spilled outside. At every corner, G.I.'s
were talking about "the blackboard," as though it provided some incontrovertible proof of the incredible. Soldiers walked, some ran, to the Rainbow Club. They would
stand for a second, then turn away. An hour after the

usual closing time of the Club, men were still arriving, breathless, not satisfied until they had seen the blackboard for themselves.

Behind the front lines in Germany, General Dwight D. Eisenhower, Supreme Commander of the Allied Forces in Europe, was concluding a conference with Generals George S. Patton and Omar Bradley in Patton's headquarters trailer. Eisenhower had spent the day inspecting the debris of the captured town of Gotha, 173 miles southwest of Berlin, where he had seen for the first time a Nazi horror camp. He had toured every corner of the camp, so that he could personally contradict rumors that "the stories of Nazi brutality were just propaganda."

Now Eisenhower said good night to Patton, and went with Bradley to retire in a small house nearby. After their departure, Patton noticed that his watch had stopped. He turned on his radio to set his watch by the opening of the midnight news broadcast from the B.B.C. The broadcast began with the explosive announcement that the American Commander in Chief was dead.

Patton raced to the house and roused Bradley. Together, they went to Eisenhower's room to convey the shocking news. For a long time, the three soldiers talked. "We were certain," Eisenhower has written, "that there would be no interference with the tempo of the war because we already knew something of the great measures afoot in the Pacific to accomplish the smashing of the Japanese. . . . But we were doubtful that there was any other individual in America as experienced as he in the business of dealing with other Allied political leaders. . . . We went to bed depressed. . . ."

In Moscow, where it was two A.M., American Ambassador W. Averell Harriman was chatting gaily with guests at an embassy party. An aide entered and handed Harri-

man a message that had just come by radio from the
Pentagon. Harriman whitened. It was clear to the guests
that, whatever the message read, the party was over.

Within an hour, Foreign Minister Vyacheslav Molotov,
in an extraordinary gesture, appeared at the embassy. He
had already brought the news to Marshal Joseph Stalin,
who now was sitting behind the pink walls of the Krem-
lin composing messages to Mrs. Roosevelt and Harry S.
Truman. Molotov said that Stalin wished to see Harriman
in the morning.

The news that created such dismay in London and Moscow created a different reaction in Berlin. The people of
that embattled city, caught in the vise of onrushing American and Soviet troops, learned of the news from D.N.B.,
the Nazi news agency. "President Roosevelt," they were
told, "will go down in history as the man upon whose
instigation the present war turned into the Second World
War." The news, acknowledged D.N.B., "has, of course,
made a great impression in Berlin."

The news had indeed made a great impression there. In
high political circles, it was even taken as a personal vindi-
cation of Joseph Goebbels, the Nazi Minister of Propaganda and National Enlightenment. A few days earlier,
according to the diary of Finance Minister Schwerin von
Krosigk, Goebbels had been soothing the nerves of Chan-
cellor Adolf Hitler by reading him a passage from Car-
lyle's *History of Frederick the Great*. The passage described the hopelessness confronting the Prussian king in
the winter of 1761-62 during the Seven Years' War. It
told how Frederick knew that, if he could hold out against
the Russians a little longer, "behind the clouds the sun of
good fortune" would rise. Sure enough, on February 12th,
the Czarina died and the military tide soon turned. The
two events, although of questionable relationship, were
described as the Miracle of the House of Brandenburg. As

Goebbels read, tears came to the Führer's eyes. Goebbels thereupon sent for a horoscope of Hitler; reading it, he predicted a great success for Germany in the latter half of April, followed by peace in August.

On April 12th, Goebbels had visited the tattered army of General Busse at Kuestrin, where he argued that a new Miracle of the House of Brandenburg was in the making. An officer asked cynically which Czarina was to die this time. Angered, Goebbels returned that night to Berlin— and there he learned of Roosevelt's death. He phoned Busse and triumphantly cried: "The Czarina is dead!" Busse was deeply impressed. Then Goebbels called for champagne and phoned Hitler. According to Frau Haberzettel, one of Goebbels' secretaries, he exclaimed: "My Führer, I congratulate you! Roosevelt is dead. It is written in the stars that the second half of April will be the turning point for us!"

So swiftly was the news flashed to distant corners of the world that it was received in Berlin, Moscow, London, Chungking, and Tokyo before it was widely known even in Georgia, from which the tremor had radiated.

On a highway near Macon, a white Cadillac convertible was speeding toward the South Carolina line. For three hours its occupants had traveled almost wordlessly. At last Mrs. Winthrop Rutherfurd turned to the driver, Madame Shoumatoff, and asked if it would be all right if she turned on the radio. Madame Shoumatoff said, "Go right ahead."

Music began to float softly from the loudspeaker. But the music eased no taut nerves in the car. The two women had seen the President of the United States collapse before their eyes. The occurrence was so awesome they had not even mentioned it to the car's third passenger, Nicholas Robbins, the photographer; nor had they dared to call

Warm Springs after their hasty departure to inquire about later developments.

The music had hardly begun to fill the conversational void when abruptly it stopped. An excited announcer said, "We interrupt this program to bring you a special bulletin. . . ." A moment later, Mrs. Rutherfurd released a painful gasp and covered her eyes.

10

"They Have
Put in a New Man"

William D. Simmons was painting the front porch of his Arlington, Virginia, home at about five-thirty in the afternoon when the telephone rang. Simmons, who was employed at the White House as the chief receptionist in the office of the President, lay down his brush and strolled inside.

The caller was Wilson Searles, a White House usher. In an oddly urgent tone, he said that Mr. Early wanted Mr. Simmons to hurry to the White House. Simmons didn't ask why; a White House employee never does. He dressed quickly, climbed into his car, turned on the radio, and headed toward the 14th Street Bridge.

A calm man who had witnessed many unexpected things, great and small, in twelve years at the White House, Simmons wasted little curiosity over the reason for his call. He'd find out when he got there and that would be soon enough. He was confident that whatever it was he had surely seen worse.

As his car neared the bridge, the music on his radio suddenly stopped. Then an agitated announcer broke in, sputtering the explosive flash.

On Simmons' stony face there was only the most subtle shift in expression, a hardening of the jawline, a deepening of the creases around the eyes. His foot pressed slightly harder on the accelerator. His mind froze—a practiced state of enforced calm—while it grappled for comprehension of the dreadful words. *So it's happened.* Simmons, a studious daily observer of Roosevelt, had known for a long time that it could happen—but he never let himself seriously consider that it would.

Then, like a thunderclap, there came a realization of why he had been called to the White House. It was perfectly obvious, yet impossible to grasp. *At the White House, they were now preparing to swear in a new man for the job.* The thought was so stunning that Simmons had to prod his mind for a puzzled instant to remember who the new man was.

Simmons had not, by any way of thinking, been a confidant of Roosevelt—but he felt close. A man can feel a special kinship with another merely because they wear the same size suit. And Simmons, a large man with powerful shoulders like those of the President himself, felt such a kinship for his boss. He could trace this feeling to an afternoon in 1936 on a campaign train in Arkansas, when Roosevelt was running for his second term. Roosevelt had summoned Simmons to his private car at the rear of the train and regarded him sternly. Then, in a voice that seemed to rise from profound considerations, Roosevelt asked: "Bill, how would you like to be President for a while?"

Simmons returned the intent look, trying to assess whether the Chief Executive had gone out of his mind.

"Only for a little while," the President went on, ignoring the widening, apprehensive eyes of Simmons. "Maybe an hour or two."

Roosevelt rolled his wheel chair away from the window and instructed Simmons to pull up a chair and sit at the vacated spot. The President removed his pince-nez glasses, pinning them on Simmons' nose, and leaned back to peer with a critical eye.

"Fine! Fine!" Roosevelt exclaimed and began to laugh uproariously. Then he announced that he was tired of sitting there waving at crowds in every passing town. With a flourish, he turned over his cigarette holder to Simmons and showed him how to wave a big, open-fingered hand in the Rooseveltian manner and how to smile a big, open-jawed smile.

"Fine! Fine!" the President said again. "Now every time we pass a town, just sit there and wave. I'm tired. I'm going to take a nap." And he wheeled out of the lounge.

All across the State of Arkansas, Simmons sat by the President's window. At each town the train slowed, not too little, nor too much; just enough so the local towns-folk could experience the incomparable thrill of seeing that fine, open-handed wave and the magnificent smile that one man, and one man alone, could thrill them with.

Simmons now lumbered into the Executive Office lobby and turned left at the first door, heading down a narrow corridor past the press secretary's office toward the Cabinet Room. This undoubtedly was where the new man was to be sworn in.

Simmons' kinship with the Boss had been strengthened in this room. It was here, in 1943, many years after the Arkansas incident, that Roosevelt again summoned Simmons and regarded him carefully. This time, instead of handing Simmons his cigarette holder and glasses, Roosevelt made him try on his famous navy cape. "Fine! Fine!" he boomed. Then he told Simmons that a portrait painter, a Madame Shoumatoff, waiting in the Cabinet Room, was in the midst of painting a Presidential portrait. The face and head were already done. The President wanted his chief receptionist to spread his broad shoulders and sit for the rest of the tedious job.

Now, in that same, serene room, members of the Cabinet were standing, pacing, smoking, whispering, imbuing the room with an air of impatient crisis. Leaders of Congress arrived. The gathering was not large, but the room seemed crowded and oppressive as new arrivals filled its corners around the long, dark Cabinet table. The table was surrounded by leather chairs; one chair, higher than the rest, and now strangely dominant and conspicuously emptier than the rest, stood at the middle of the table's length, its back to the rear wall.

Secretary of State Stettinius was a portrait of stiff control at the edge of explosion. Labor Secretary Frances Perkins—"Madame Secretary," everyone called her—was weeping freely into a handkerchief. Secretary of Commerce Wallace wore an uncharacteristic, dark frown, and was uncharacteristically wordless. Secretary of the Interior Harold Ickes worked his lips and paced. The aging Secretary of War, Henry Stimson, could be seen rushing down the hall toward the room. He was murmuring to himself, his fist crushing the brim of his hat. As reporters stepped toward him, he waved the hat impatiently as though to swat them away.

Harry S. Truman entered.

There was some shaking of hands; few words. Simmons asked Mr. Truman if he thought Mrs. Truman and their daughter Margaret would like to witness the ceremony.

"Why yes," Mr. Truman said, faintly surprised, "I guess they would."

Simmons said he would order a car. Mr. Truman headed for a telephone. He told the operator to get his home.

In a five-room apartment on the second floor of 4701 Connecticut Avenue, Mary Margaret Truman, a twenty-year-old college student, was dressing for a date—dinner and the theater—with Marvin Braverman, a new beau. Afterwards, they were to return to the apartment building for the birthday party of Annette Davis Wright, the daughter of General and Mrs. Jeff Davis, the Trumans' next-door neighbors.

When the phone rang, Margaret answered and, with the winged cheeriness of a co-ed about to fly off on a date, said, "Hi, Dad." She has recalled that her father's voice sounded "tight and funny."

He said: "Let me speak to your mother."

"Are you coming home for dinner?" she asked.

"Let me speak to your mother."

"I only asked a civil question," Margaret pouted.

"*Margaret, will you let me speak to your mother.*"

Offended, she called her mother and returned to making up her face.

A moment later, Mrs. Truman was standing at Margaret's door. She seemed to be trembling, but she wasn't. She seemed about to speak, but she was mute. She stared at Margaret, but seemed not to see.

"Mother, what's the matter? What is it?"

"President Roosevelt is dead."

"*Dead?*"

After a long pause, Mrs. Truman said, "You better change your clothes. And call Marvin."

Mrs. Truman, struggling to hold her composure, dialed the telephone of her apartment house manager and close

friend, Mrs. Oscar J. Ricketts. When Mrs. Ricketts arrived she found Mrs. Truman fully surrendered to shock
and grief.

The doorbell rang. Margaret ran to answer and found a
young lady there.

"Miss Truman?"

"Yes."

"I'm from the Associated Press. I would like a . . ."

Margaret realized she had answered the door in her slip.

"I can't talk to you now," she blurted out, shutting,
almost slamming, the door. Suddenly she felt angry, in-
truded upon.

"It was the last time," Miss Truman has said, "I ever
opened a door without finding out who was there. . . .
At that moment I ceased to be a free agent."

Margaret dressed quickly in a brown suit, the only appropriate garment she had that was pressed.

A crowd was gathering on the front lawn of the apartment building. As the Truman women stepped out of their
elevator, camera bulbs flashed from all directions. They
were led by Secret Service men through a back door to a
White House limousine, and they sped down Connecticut
Avenue. Arriving at the White House, they entered the
residential quarters to visit Mrs. Roosevelt.

In the Cabinet Room, the solemn-faced men who en-
gineered the business of the Republic were waiting for the
ceremony to begin. Now all the members of the Cabinet
were there, except for Postmaster General Frank Walker,
who had been caught by the news in Lynchburg, Virginia.
Fred M. Vinson, the Director of Economic Stabilization,
chatted quietly with his former colleagues in the House of
Representatives: Speaker Rayburn, Majority Leader John
W. McCormack, Democratic Whip Robert Ramspeck, and
Minority Leader Joseph W. Martin, Jr.

During the pause, one Cabinet member performed what

was probably the first act in the subtle realignment of governmental power that was inevitably to dominate the action of the next few days. Secretary of the Navy James Forrestal quietly put in a call to Spartanburg, South Carolina, for James F. Byrnes. Byrnes, whom many believed to be embittered because he failed to win Roosevelt's support for the Vice-Presidential nomination, had resigned as War Mobilization Director two weeks earlier. (When Roosevelt at Warm Springs was signing a letter accepting Byrnes's resignation, Bill Hassett remarked that the resignation meant a loss to Roosevelt and the government. "Yes," Roosevelt replied wearily. "It's too bad some people are so prima-donnaish.")

Forrestal suggested to Byrnes that he come to Washington immediately, and offered to send a Navy plane to fetch him. Byrnes quickly accepted the offer. Then Forrestal told the incoming President that Byrnes was on his way to Washington. Truman said that was fine and that he wanted to see Byrnes first thing in the morning.

The Chief Justice of the Supreme Court, Harlan F. Stone, waited nervously while Bill Simmons moved from office to office, rummaging through desk drawers and shelves. Simmons was searching all through the White House Executive Wing for a Bible. Then he remembered once having seen one in Hassett's office, an inexpensive, red-edged Thomas Nelson and Sons edition, which he believed Hassett used to check the accuracy of quotations. (Hassett says it was a recent gift that he had not yet had a chance to acknowledge.) Simmons brought the volume to the Cabinet Room and explained apologetically to Mr. Truman that it was the only Bible he could find. Mr. Truman said it would be perfectly all right.

Now the Cabinet Room was swarming with photographers who seemed to have seized control. They ordered the keepers of the Republic about, and the keepers of the

Republic dutifully obeyed, posing in this grouping and that.

A few minutes after seven, Mrs. Truman and Margaret entered. Mrs. Truman was red-eyed. She looked frightened.

The room hushed. For the first time in twelve years, a new man was about to pledge himself to guide the destiny of the United States of America. For the seventh time in the life of the nation, as the body of a President awaited burial, another man, exhumed from a job called "a political graveyard," was to be thrust abruptly into imponderable power.

Chief Justice Harlan F. Stone and Harry S. Truman faced each other. Stone, aging, benign-faced, wore a blue serge suit. There had been no time to procure a robe of judicial sanctity. Truman wore a gray suit, white shirt, and polka-dot tie. He lifted the Bible from the Cabinet table. He held it in his left hand and covered it with his right. Truman seemed to be staring hard through his thick glasses. His lips were firm. He stood erect.

From memory, Chief Justice Stone began: "I, Harry Shippe Truman, . . ."

Mr. Truman responded: "I, Harry S. Truman, . . ." (Mr. Truman's middle initial is often believed to have been taken from his paternal grandfather, Anderson Shippe Truman. The "S," however, stands for no name at all.)

". . . do solemnly swear that I will faithfully execute the office of President of the United States, and will, to the best of my ability, preserve, protect, and defend the Constitution of the United States."

Then Stone said: "So help you God."

Truman said: "So help me God."

At the door, the beefy fist of a man plunged into the air. It was startling, almost like a Communist salute. It was the fist of Arthur Hermann of International News Service, a signal to Felix Cotten of I.N.S. who was watching for it down the hall in the lobby of the Executive Wing. Cotten's arm shot into the air, a signal to another I.N.S. man around a corner at the door of the press room. His arm, in turn, punched the air, a signal to a reporter at the I.N.S. private phone.

"Truman sworn in!" the reporter shouted.

Meanwhile, two less provident reporters from the competing wire services were trying to scramble through the jammed lobby to get to their phones.

At the I.N.S. bureau office, Jean Van Vranken, a phone pressed to her ear, was waiting for the word. When it came, it came like the blow of a hammer. She was startled. Until now, it had been a news story; the office bedlam merely a drama. *But now they have put in a new man. The beginning is an ending. The President is really lying dead.*

"When Jean yelled, 'Flash—Truman sworn in!' I never saw such a look on anyone's face in my life," says Betsy Tupman, the dictation girl. "She looked at the ceiling, caught her lip in between her teeth, and didn't breathe again until the story was well on the wire."

In the Cabinet Room, the swearing-in was being repeated on the demand of a loud, elbowing mob of photographers. Under a portrait of Woodrow Wilson and over the head of the new President, a clock pointed to 7:09. President Roosevelt had been dead for two hours and thirty-four minutes. Steve Early, conferring hastily with photographers and reporters, decided that to guarantee the authenticity of the photographs, 7:09 would be recorded as the official time of the swearing-in. The I.N.S. flash, transmitted seconds after Truman took his first oath, had been timed at 7:08.

After the ceremony, Mrs. Truman and Margaret quickly left for home. The assembled officials began to withdraw. Each shook the hand of the new President, some without a word. Soon, only the members of the Cabinet were left.

They seated themselves around the table, each in his accustomed place. With the disappearance of the flash bulbs, the room now seemed curiously subdued. Two chairs were empty—the Postmaster General's, and the Vice-President's opposite the high one of the President. In the President's chair sat Harry S. Truman. The grave individuals around the table each labored privately at making the elusive adjustment in his mind, that this was how it was now going to be. And each wondered just *how* it was now going to be.

The new President was about to speak when Jonathan Daniels, the press secretary, bustled into the room. Daniels said that the press was demanding to know if the San Francisco conference would go on as scheduled on April 25th. Members of the Roosevelt Cabinet, some of whom had not known Harry Truman intimately, sharpened their focus on the new leader. This was no minor query that Daniels had posed.

With a remarkable absence of hesitation, the man with the thick glasses said—as though he thought the matter were simple—that the conference *had* to take place as President Roosevelt had directed. The conference was of supreme importance, he instructed Daniels to say, to help keep the future peace of the world.

Something in the tone of the room changed.

Then Truman addressed his department heads. As he had already told some of them individually, he said he wished they would all remain in their posts. It was his intention, he said, to continue the domestic and foreign policies of the Roosevelt administration. He emphasized, however, that he would be President in his own right, fully responsible for his decisions. He would seek the advice of his Cabinet, and its members should feel free to differ with him when necessary, but all final decisions would be his. Once decisions were made, Truman said, he expected his Cabinet to support them. The coming of a new President, he said, was bound to bring changes in the Cabinet, but he expected to keep an open mind concerning all members until they had had an opportunity to work together. (A short while later, Secretary Ickes told a reporter, with a shading of surprise and perhaps relief, "I believe he meant it.")

The short meeting was over.

The Cabinet members rose and silently filed out of the room—all except Secretary of War Stimson.

Stimson, grim-faced and speaking in a guarded, low tone, said he had a most urgent matter to bring to the President's attention. Truman invited him to sit down. The Secretary said the President should know of an immense project that was under way, of which only a handful of people knew. It was a project for developing a new explosive of almost unbelievable destructive power. That was all, the Secretary said, he felt equipped to say at the moment. The statement left Truman puzzled; but it explained something.

Many months before, Truman had got wind, as head of the Senate war investigating committee, that something uncommonly big, expensive, and mysterious was going on in the states of Tennessee and Washington. He sent investigators to check. Soon, Secretary Stimson phoned Senator Truman and urged a private talk. Truman volunteered to come to Stimson's office at once. Stimson said no, he would come to see the Senator.

Stimson gingerly but emphatically asked Truman to call his investigators off. "Senator, I can't tell you what it is," he said, according to Truman, "but it is the greatest project in the history of the world. It is most top secret. Many of the people who are actually engaged in the work have no idea what it is, and we who do would appreciate your not going into those plants."

Truman, taking Stimson at his word, pulled his investigators out. Later, Truman was to say it was "a miracle" that so vast an enterprise as the making of the atomic bomb had been kept a secret even from key members of Congress.

When the conversation with Stimson ended, Truman strode through the lobby of the Executive Wing to his waiting car. The car, now part of a procession, moved out the south gate and pointed up Connecticut Avenue.

In the lobby, Bill Simmons stood up at his desk to drone the traditional day's-end announcement, which on this day had a curious ring: "The President has left his office."

At 4701 Connecticut Avenue, the birthday party for Margaret's neighbor, Annette Davis Wright, had been cancelled. Her parents, General and Mrs. Davis, brought most of the food into the Truman apartment. Mrs. Truman and Margaret were nibbling at birthday cake when the new President of the United States came home and sank wearily into a dining-room chair.

He had eaten nothing since noon. Mrs. Davis fixed him a ham-and-turkey sandwich and a glass of milk. After his hasty meal, the President announced that he had a big day ahead of him tomorrow and was going right to bed. Just before turning in, however, he paused to place a telephone call to Missouri.

In the little town of Grandview, Missouri, Mrs. Martha Truman was sitting anxiously near her radio, not wanting to miss anything. All evening her doorbell and phone had been jangling with calls from newspaper reporters. Each time, her son Vivian had politely declined to call his ninety-one-year-old mother, explaining that she is "in good health and we want to keep it that way."

But Mrs. Truman did come to the phone when her son in Washington called.

"Mama," he said, "I'm terribly busy." He assured her, however, that everything was all right and that he was confident of the future. He added, trusting she would understand: "You probably won't hear from me for some time."

While the head of the new administration lay asleep in his modest Washington apartment, a grim committee of six had gathered in the quiet of the White House to transact the final business of the old administration. They were planning the funeral of Franklin D. Roosevelt.

Earlier, A. B. Tolley and Edith Helm of the White House Social Bureau had searched their files for records of the funeral of Warren G. Harding, the last President to have died in office. But the files were gone. According to custom, they had been given to Mrs. Harding. So, with no precedents at hand to guide the making of their uncommon plans, Tolley and Mrs. Helm sat down to counsel with Jonathan Daniels; George T. Summerlin, the Chief of Protocol of the State Department; Major Henry Hooker, a friend of the Roosevelts who had been staying at the White House; and Malvina Thompson, Mrs. Roosevelt's secretary. Later they were joined by Anna Roosevelt Boettiger and her husband.

The committee took up its most difficult problem first: whom to invite to the funeral. The East Room would hold only two hundred. They agreed to let the State Department choose a number of chiefs of diplomatic missions (but not their wives). Invitations would go to the Cabinet, the Supreme Court, heads of independent agencies, fourteen members of the White House press corps, and certain close friends of the family.

Tolley produced a list of guests at the 1936 funeral of

Roosevelt's campaign adviser, Louis Howe. Miss Thompson said it was a valuable list of old political friends. Then someone thought of examining the guest list of the 1945 inauguration. Miss Thompson added that she thought James A. Farley ought to be invited. (The friendship between Roosevelt and Farley had broken when the President decided to run for a third term.) It was agreed.

By this time a messenger had come from Summerlin's office at the State Department with a copy of the engraved invitation to the Harding funeral. Summerlin traced it, noted changes to be made, and at eleven P.M. went to the Government Printing Office near the Capitol, ordering that cards be ready at 9 A.M. Friday. The invitation was to be embossed with the Presidential crest, and was to read:

Funeral Services
of
FRANKLIN DELANO ROOSEVELT
Late President of the United States
April fourteenth, Nineteen Hundred and Forty-Five
at four o'clock p.m.
The East Room
The White House

When the meeting ended, Jonathan Daniels went to the Executive Wing to perform a final task for the night. With Bill Simmons, he entered the President's office. Almost half of the desk top was cluttered with dozens of trinkets and curios—china dolls, toy elephants, tiny ship models—that Franklin Roosevelt had fondly collected over the years. These they carefully wrapped and packed into boxes. Later, these mementoes were distributed to those who had worked with Franklin Roosevelt and would cherish the trinkets he had left behind. Simmons received a linen handkerchief embroidered with the President's initials; Daniels, a wooden paperweight carved to form the letters F.D.R.

11

"He Made
a Way for Folks"

"There has not been time to think," said Robert Trout on the C.B.S. network at 11:10 P.M. "The news is known but the brain does not quite grasp it. There is the knowledge that in the days to come the loss will be felt often, at various turns in the road. The mind knows that, for that is the way of death. But the mind does not wish to consider it in all its implications, not yet. . . ."

Ever since the news had begun to spread, however, the minds of various men had indeed been struggling to consider its implications. Few minds anywhere dwelt on anything else.

At 7:45, Ned Calmer of C.B.S., his voice unsteady, had read the first statements of public men. They were by Herbert Hoover, Thomas E. Dewey, Norman Thomas, Winston Churchill, Ellis Arnall, and Frank Hague. By no one's design, this first group of utterances symbolized the broad political tapestry that F.D.R. had succeeded in knitting together for a time of war: two Republicans he had crushed at the polls, one old, one young; America's leading Socialist; Britain's leader of the Conservatives; a Southern governor; and a Northern big city machine boss.

Other statements, as they were scribbled by harried reporters, recorded usually eloquent officials in a rare state—they were almost at a loss for words.

"I am too shocked to talk. It is one of the worst tragedies that ever happened. . . ." That was Senate Majority Leader Barkley.

Speaker Sam Rayburn, "too shocked and flustered" to say anything, chose instead to write a few words for a reporter: "We know not how to interpret God in the way He performs. . . ."

One official never at a loss for words, not even now, was Fiorello H. La Guardia, New York City's fiery, emotional mayor. He flicked on a microphone at his desk and addressed the people extemporaneously over the city-owned radio station W.N.Y.C., his voice shaking as he pounded the desk: "Franklin Roosevelt is not dead. His ideals live. That pattern is so definite. It is so permanent. We cannot escape it. We must not escape it. We do not want to escape it. We cannot avoid it and we will not avoid it. Centuries and centuries from now, as long as history is recorded, people will know Franklin Delano Roosevelt loved humanity. I call upon all New Yorkers to carry on!"

Reporters sought statements from those who had spent their political careers battling against Roosevelt. Senator Robert A. Taft, the man who had come to be called "Mr. Republican," who was seldom unreserved in his criticism of F.D.R., was now surprisingly unreserved in his tribute: "The President's death removes the greatest figure of our time at the very climax of his career, and shocks the world to which his words and actions were more important than those of any other man. He dies a hero of the

war, for he literally worked himself to death in the service
of the American people."

Some tributes approached the embarrassing. Mayor
Cooper Green of Birmingham, Alabama, predicted that
Roosevelt would become known as "the world's greatest
humanitarian since the life of Christ." To Senator Clyde
R. Hoey, a Democrat from North Carolina, who was perhaps less impressed, the news was "as severe a shock as
this nation has sustained since the assassination of President McKinley."

As such quotations poured across news desks, reporters
worked furiously to rush them into print. But in the more
staid offices of editorial writers, men probed their minds
for cooler appraisals of what had occurred. Editorial
writers are usually among the most unexcitable of men.
But now even the studied restraint of those at the New
York *Times* seemed to have been swept away:

"Men will thank God on their knees, a hundred years
from now, that Franklin D. Roosevelt was in the White
House . . . in that dark hour when a powerful and ruth-
less barbarism threatened to overrun the civilization of
the Western World. . . . It was his hand, more than that
of any other single man, that built the great coalition of
the United Nations. It was his genius for finding ways of
accommodating apparently irreconcilable opinions that
held this coalition together in the hard days of frustration
and defeat. It was his leadership which inspired free men
in every part of the world to fight with greater hope and
courage.

"Gone, now, is this talent and skill. . . . Gone is the
exuberance and the enthusiasm and the indomitable courage that conquered the hardest of personal afflictions.
. . . Gone is the fresh and spontaneous interest which
this man took, as naturally as he breathed air, in the trou-

bles and the hardships and the disappointments and the hopes of little men and humble people. . . ."

In Chicago a Republican newspaper, the *Daily News*, similarly forsook restraint:

"So overwhelming was his personality that, in effect, it killed two political parties, leaving both without orthodox creeds or dynamic leaders. So close did he become to the masses, and so high did his spirit vault ancient political barriers that millions of voters became independents." The editorial also said: "He hadn't done all he had hoped to do. He had had to compromise. He said he knew that he hadn't reached perfectionism. But . . . we like to think of him passing into the Valley of the Shades to rest not far from another leader who also died just before his followers came to the land of promise—Moses."

While newspapers sought to evaluate Roosevelt against the long perspective of human history, a young soldier, writing an editorial for *Yank, The Army Weekly*, took on a simpler task. In behalf of his youthful buddies around the world, he wrote of recent history he had personally known, symbolized by a man who, in a sense, he had also personally known:

"Most of us in the Army have a hard time remembering any President but Franklin D. Roosevelt. We never saw the inside of a speakeasy, because he had prohibition repealed before we were old enough to drink. When we were kids during the depression, and the factories and the stores were not taking anybody, plenty of us joined the CCCs, and the hard work in the woods felt good after those months of sleeping late and hanging around the house and the corner drug store, too broke to go anywhere and do anything. Or we got our first jobs on his ERA and WPA projects. That seems like a long time ago.

". . . we made cracks about Roosevelt and told Roosevelt jokes and sometimes we bitterly criticized his way of doing things. But he was still Roosevelt, the man we had grown up under. . . . He was the Commander-in-Chief, not only of the armed forces, but of our generation.

"That is why it is hard to realize he is dead, even in these days when death is a common and expected thing."

While the young soldier on *Yank* reminisced about the projects of the W.P.A., a columnist syndicated by the New York *Post*, Samuel Grafton, was spurred on the night of Roosevelt's death to justify them:

"Leaf-raking was silly. You cannot tell me he did not know it was silly. He knew. But as against a concentration camp, it was noble. As against what happened in Spain, leaf-raking even had grandeur. I think he knew these things, and there was a knowledge of them in his smile when he was attacked and baited.

"He had no answers that were good for a hundred years. But in a six-month crisis he always had a six-month answer. . . . Maybe he had a right to smile, and to think that a billion was not so much; maybe he knew what he had got for it, and that it was a bargain."

Chatting with a reporter that night, an aged Georgia Negro named Nelson Waters put it more simply: "He made a way for folks when there wasn't no way."

It was an hour when each individual seemed moved to summarize his own connection with the piece of history that had so abruptly ended. Robert Trout went on the air again, with no script, for some leisurely reminiscences as one who had introduced Roosevelt on the radio from the White House and traveled with him across the land:

"Once as I was describing to Columbia's radio audience the approach of the President up the ramp to the speakers' platform at one of the largest political rallies of all, the braces of his legs gave way and he fell. The pages of his

manuscript were scattered. They were picked up by willing hands and hurriedly handed back to the President, who
by that time had been seated—now within view of the
audience of many thousands. He put the pages together
as best he could in the few minutes before he was introduced. The manuscript was damp, crumpled, and spattered
with mud. It was a tense moment and Roosevelt did not
falter. Only a handful of the thousands in the stadium that
night had the faintest idea that anything at all had gone
wrong. That was the night the President, in a strong and
confident voice, proclaimed, 'This generation has a rendezvous with destiny.'

". . . That memorable Sunday in 1933 when the new
President was to broadcast the proclamation closing the
nation's banks . . . the White House corridors were still
cluttered with baggage and packing cases. The first family
of the land had not yet had time to unpack and move in.
. . . A few minutes before air time, it was discovered
that the manuscript for the first Fireside Chat was missing. A search was made for the missing speech, amidst
great excitement. But one man was untouched by the excitement—Mr. Roosevelt. He was unperturbed and seemed
perfectly satisfied when someone found a mimeographed
press copy of the speech. It was not so easy a copy to read,
especially to so large an audience at a time so tense, but
the President used that copy when he spoke. His cigarette,
in the long ivory holder, burned down nearly to the end
as he talked on the air. I watched it in strained fascination,
for in those days in Washington, radio reporters in Washington were not so used to statesmen who felt so thoroughly at home before a microphone that they could
stamp out a cigarette in an ash tray while broadcasting,
without pausing or stumbling. . . . Franklin Roosevelt
was not upset during that broadcast or any of the others
when unplanned incidents occurred, such as on the night

when his son, James, stepped without looking and fell over the President's wheel chair with a loud crash just as I had finished the introduction and Mr. Roosevelt started to speak. . . .

"There were many strange, and often moving, sights to be seen on the Presidential trips across the country. . . . Once in the rugged country of Idaho, we had roared along in the train for many miles without seeing a house or a man. Suddenly, the train raced out from between the tall trees, and ran beside a quiet mountain lake. There on a tiny, homemade pier, beside his log cabin, stood a man—a trapper or a fisherman or a hunter perhaps—standing on his little pier, between two large American flags he had rigged up, standing at attention, with his hand in a military salute at his forehead as the train sped past. He had made his arrangements, put up his decorations, and he greeted the train for the few moments it was visible to him."

As individuals felt the need to commemorate in some personal way the passing of the President, even impersonal institutions were moved to act. But instead of finding something special to do, they reacted by finding something not to do. The broadcasting networks cancelled all commercials. The New York *Times*, the *Herald Tribune*, the *Daily News*, and other papers across the country cancelled all advertising of merchandise for their Friday editions. Night clubs closed their doors. The New York Philharmonic Symphony Orchestra cancelled its concert at Carnegie Hall. This was the second time in its long history it had done so. The first time was on the occasion of Abraham Lincoln's death.

12

"Going Home"

"A massive cerebral hemorrhage," Dr. Bruenn had said, when the reporters asked him the cause of death.

Massive.

To the doctor who used it, the word was merely clinical. But to a world of laymen, the word rang a resounding, shuddering truth.

The actual occurrence that had shaken the world, as the doctor might have explained if the reporters had pressed for more details, was the appearance of a tiny break in a thin tube through which the patient's life blood flowed—a brain artery. At first, the hole may have been the size of a pinpoint. The artery perhaps had grown a tiny sac that burst; or, no longer young, the artery had become brittle and had cracked. The fluid trickled into spaces around the brain.

The brain, a sheltered and tender instrument, responsive to the smallest irregularity, sent out urgent messages of pain. The eyes grew dull; the body dizzy. The heart, reacting to a leakage of valuable fluid somewhere in the system, stepped up the pumping pressure. Soon the body sought to shut off all unnecessary drains on its strength: it turned off the lights of consciousness. But the leakage continued. Finally the body, incapable of coping with the emergency, stopped functioning altogether.

In a way which was not at all uncommon, the life of a man had come to a natural end. But such a natural occurrence, even in a land where it is said that all men are created equal, can disarrange the vast and hardy mechanism of society. For even if all men are equal when they are created, they are not always equal when they die.

Because the preservation of Franklin Roosevelt's life had been important to his country, more important than that of other men, members of the United States Marine Corps —hidden in sentry boxes around his cottage at Warm Springs—had guarded him day and night. Now, even though the life had slipped away, they still kept watch, halting the curious who gathered outside, protecting the privacy of those in the cottage who now had unexpected tasks to perform.

Bill Hassett had to buy a coffin. He was entirely without experience for the job, but Steve Early had just called him from Washington saying Mrs. Roosevelt trustfully had put the mission in Hassett's hands. Hassett asked Grace Tully for an opinion on its style. Miss Tully could only say that she was sure the Boss would want something simple and dignified. Dr. Bruenn agreed.

On the recommendation of Dr. Paullin, Hassett phoned the funeral parlors of H. M. Patterson and Son in Atlanta. Fred Patterson, the owner, had already been alerted by Dr. Paullin to expect the call. Hassett said he wanted a solid mahogany casket with a copper lining. Patterson told him that copper linings had disappeared early in the war. He did have, however, a plain mahogany one, but . . .

Hassett broke in to ask if it were at least six feet four inches long. Patterson said it was—but it was already sold. It was to be shipped the next day to New Jersey to accommodate another undertaker. He added that he had a fine bronze-colored copper model that would . . . Hassett, in his gentle but most firm Vermont manner, said he wanted the mahogany brought at once to Warm Springs. Patterson asked if he could bring both. Perhaps, on reconsideration, they would choose the bronze-colored copper one. Hassett said he could.

Patterson and four assistants drove to Warm Springs in a car and two hearses, arriving at 10:45. They were told that the body was not to be touched until Mrs. Roosevelt arrived. She was about now landing at Fort Benning.

At 11:25, Mrs. Roosevelt, who had been traveling from Washington for more than five hours, entered the cottage with Steve Early and Ross McIntire. She appeared calm. Miss Delano, Miss Suckley, and Miss Tully each embraced and kissed her. Miss Tully said, "You know how sorry I am for you and the children."

Mrs. Roosevelt touched her shoulder and said, "Tully dear, I am so very sorry for all of you."

The widow sat on the sofa and asked each of the cousins and Miss Tully to tell exactly what had happened. Then she rose and walked to the bedroom, closing the door behind her. For five minutes she was alone with her husband. When she came out, her face was grave, eyes dry.

Patterson, the undertaker, recalls: "After Mrs. Roosevelt had seen the President's remains, a conference was held as to funeral arrangements. I asked Dr. Bruenn what they wished to do about the casket. He consulted Dr. McIntire. . . . In the conversation, the Admiral was heard to use the word 'bronze' and as the copper deposit had a bronze finish, of course that was the casket to be used."

At the Warm Springs railroad depot, a crowd had been gathering. The stars were bright, air thick with honeysuckle perfume.

"An hour after the news first broke," Station Agent Pless recalls, "the newspapers and radio stations got folks there. One broadcasting station set up south of my depot against the road, one in front between the office and the tracks, one in the colored waiting room, two in the shed between the colored waiting room and the baggage room. The crowd kept building and milling. All of a sudden, the woods was full of folks, hundreds of them. It looked like people just fell out of the sky."

When someone talked, it was in whispers, hand over mouth. The radio had said Mrs. Roosevelt was coming to Warm Springs, and the people hoped to catch a glimpse of her. Then word came that she had already arrived at the Foundation—that she had come by plane. The crowd moved slowly across the tracks and into the lobby of the Warm Springs Hotel.

Under a portrait of Roosevelt, reporters slumped on the lobby sofa. They kept looking at their watches, impatient for word that they would be admitted to the Foundation grounds. One of them overheard an excited woman in a phone booth shouting to a distant friend, "Yes, I was just driving through town. Boy, what a thrill this is!"

Frank Allcorn walked sadly into the lobby and held up his hands for attention. The crowd listened.

"The President and his party," he said, "were to have attended a barbecue at four o'clock, and they came and told us he died. We had all the food prepared. You may come and eat it if you're hungry, or it will only go to waste." At first, nobody moved. Then Allcorn said, "It's on the house."

In the Pine Room of the Hotel, Jess Long, who had helped prepare the food at Allcorn's barbecue pit at dawn, supervised the buffet serving of Brunswick stew, lamb, pork, beef, and salads.

At 1:25 A.M. those at the station, still waiting for they knew not what, were rewarded for their long vigil. The train that had borne the President here and was now to bear him away, stole, with whispered chugs, into the station. It had come in backward; one engine tugging at the train's rear, two others pushing at its front end. In the morning, the pair in front would be in position to pull it northward.

Floodlights were turned on. Those who had often seen the train now observed that a shuffling had occurred among its eleven cars. The President's lounge and bedroom car, the *Ferdinand Magellan*, usually at the end of the train, was now second from the last. It had been transposed with the *Conneaut*, his office car. While the crowd watched, workmen entered the *Conneaut* and stripped its interior. All they left was a round mirror on the wall.

At the Little White House, where the body to be carried away in this car now rested, the undertakers had been told they could proceed with their work. One of them, Haden Snoderly, recalls: "At 12:35 A.M. we were admitted to prepare the remains. Upon entering the room, which was very small, we found the President on his bed with sheet and counterpane over his face. Apparently he had lost considerable weight. We placed the remains on our operating table. One of the Marine guards and the President's valet stayed in the room to assist us."

Fred Patterson: "As the President died at 3:35 and the embalming started at 12:35, there was a lapse of nine hours, which had already given me a great deal of concern. On starting the embalming it was shortly discovered that he had been a victim of arteriosclerosis which seemed to have seriously affected all of his arteries. . . .

"While our assistants were proceeding with the preparation it was found that the funeral train was to leave the next morning at 10 o'clock and . . . no provision had been made for a casket bier or anything on which to place the casket. I asked one of the Secret Service men if the Marine Corps, who guarded the President, had a carpenter. After some time, he brought Hoke Shipp who discussed the making of two pedestals. It was finally decided, however, to make a bier in the form of a very strong table, two inches longer than the casket and two inches wider, of Georgia pine, twenty inches high, with a molding around the top to prevent the casket from slipping. The casket dimensions were eighty-four inches long and twenty-eight inches wide. As the finish of the casket was bronze, it was decided to use two Marine blankets of a green-brown color to drape the bier."

Hoke S. "Red" Shipp, the Foundation's executive housekeeper, awoke his staff carpenter, A. G. Moody, and brought him to a cache of pine timber that had been cut the previous year on the Foundation land. It was such fine timber that Shipp had decided one day to save it for something special. Then Shipp drove to the barracks of the Marine detachment for the two blankets. The supply sergeant asked Shipp when the blankets would be returned. Shipp said they probably would not be. The sergeant, knowing of no provision in the rule book for issuing blankets for Presidential funerals, objected. Shipp said he would ask the commanding officer.

"You can't do that," the sergeant protested, "he's asleep."

"I'll wake him," Shipp threatened.

Faced with this even greater crisis, the sergeant relented.

"I went back to the President's room," Patterson recalls, "to see how the preparation was progressing, and while standing by the door, felt someone turn the knob. On opening the door, I found Mrs. Roosevelt who said she wanted to see the President and thought that we were done. I told her that I would call her later when we had finished. . . . After I had gone over different plans with the Secret Service men and had seen the bier which had been built, we returned to the Little White House and found, at 5:45, that the preparation had been completed.

"Previously, Mrs. Roosevelt had selected one of the President's double-breasted blue business suits flecked with gray, a soft white shirt with collar attached, black socks, and a dark blue-and-white four-in-hand which the valet said the President wore when he was inaugurated in 1941. These were put on the President, who was placed on his bed. We were at a loss to know what to do about a counterpane or robe. I remembered the President's navy cape. We draped it over the lower part of his body as you have seen him in pictures with his cape over his knees.

"All of us then left the room, and Mrs. Roosevelt was informed he could be seen. After she had been with him a few minutes, she came out of his room and most graciously expressed her thanks to me for everything that had been done. I believe she was the only person beside the valet, Arthur Prettyman, who saw the remains after being dressed, other than our assistants. The President was then immediately placed in the casket, which was left at the south end of the living room on a hook rug, with the lid half open and half of the inner lid closed.

"The valet was very kind to us. He served coffee about two o'clock in the morning and then again after we had finished our work. . . ."

At two-thirty A.M., Bill Hassett went to Carver Cottage to lie awake most of the night. Admiral McIntire, Steve

Early, and Dr. Bruenn went to bed in the train. All night
they heard the hum-hum-hum of trucks carrying soldiers
from Fort Benning over the mountain crest and down the
long grade into the village. At dawn, the trucks were still
coming.

By nine in the morning, Hassett, Early, McIntire, and
Bruenn were back at the Little White House. Lizzie Mc-
Duffie recalls: "They had the casket lying open in the
living room near the President's bedroom door. There
was a glass over him. Oh, he was handsome. You wouldn't
have thought he had a day's illness."

Hassett: "I stood beside Mrs. Roosevelt—almost on the
spot where the President worked at his table before the
fireplace yesterday—when the coffin was carried out by
noncoms from the various services of the armed forces. I
did not look at the face of the dead. I doubt if Mrs. Roosevelt did either. I had worked with him for the last time in
this room less than twenty-four hours earlier."

Patterson: "I was rather concerned at the last minute
because I heard that the casket was going to be taken on a
caisson to the station. About a mile of the road was not
paved, only surfaced, and the other mile was rather rough.
As the caisson did not arrive at the last minute the casket
was placed in our Sayers and Scoville Cadillac hearse.

"The time had now reached nine o'clock. . . . About
two thousand soldiers were assembled ahead of the hearse
ready to march, but no pallbearers had come. And there
was no flag for covering the casket. I requested one of our
assistants to make inquiry. Shortly, he returned, as the pallbearers came through the grounds, stating that the flag
had been given to one of the Secret Service men and could
not be found. In the middle of the grounds was a flagpole
from which the flag was immediately lowered. . . . Dust
was shaken from the flag and it was draped on the casket."

At 9:25, the slow, stately procession began to move

along a winding, red clay road down the mountainside. At its head, the United States Army Band of Fort Benning marched with precise, measured steps. Their gleaming instruments were tucked underarm; only the drums played —a relentless, muffled, rhythmic, accented roll. Behind them marched one thousand carbine-bearing infantrymen in three companies, black streamers flying from their colors.

Next came the hearse.

Behind it in a closed car, Mrs. Roosevelt sat stiffly, wearing a fur cape, the Scottie, Fala, curled at her feet. With her rode Margaret Suckley, Laura Delano, and Grace Tully. Cars bearing others in the party followed.

The procession moved between two lines of helmeted paratroopers, standing close at present arms on each side of the road like endless, winding picket fences, their faces frozen in military attention. Now and then, almost hidden by a severe, low helmet and raised rifle, tears slid down a boy's face. One soldier swayed slightly as the hearse rolled by, then caved in and gently rolled off the shoulder of the road into a ditch.

The morning air was pleasant, in the high seventies. But the sun glowed fiercely. In the branches of the trees, birds chirped.

At Georgia Hall, a great crowd waited before the majestic white columns. Always, on leaving Warm Springs, F.D.R. drove by Georgia Hall to wave good-bye to the patients and staff. Mrs. Roosevelt had asked this morning that the tradition be observed. Many were on crutches, some in wheel chairs, a few in rolling beds. They could hear the procession, the solemn crunch of feet on gravel and clay, before they could see it.

Roosevelt had known many of these patients by name. Jane Richcreek and Helen Roberts were there, Lieutenant Barry Parkell and Seaman Larry Waterman, Bernice Burns and Nancy Karsh. They had shared Thanksgiving turkey with him. At Thanksgiving, Roosevelt always carved, then he would talk and, no matter what he'd talk about, there would be lots of laughs.

A few remembered as far back as the Thanksgiving of 1934, when Roosevelt was suddenly moved to recount how the Foundation had come to be. Dr. Robert W. Lovett, who had been treating Roosevelt in Boston in 1924, mentioned one day that some of his patients swam in the warm waters of Buzzards Bay and Long Island Sound, and they seemed to show more improvement than those who went to the North Shore or the coast of Maine, where they could not stand the cold temperatures for more than three or four minutes at a time. Later, Roosevelt received a letter from Tom Loyless, a friend in Warm Springs, telling of a paralyzed boy who had spent hours in the inviting, warm waters of a natural pool and had taught himself to walk, first in the buoyancy of the water, finally on dry land.

"Well, I put two and two together," Roosevelt told the Thanksgiving diners, "and I said to myself this confirms Lovett's theory. . . . We came down in the autumn. The only people who were here when we arrived were Mr. and Mrs. Loyless and old Mr. Watts, a postman, and it is perfectly true that he read everybody's post cards. In fact, he read so many post cards that it took him almost all day to make the delivery of the mail to the Loyless cottage and mine.

"When we came down, there was no doctor around here. There was nobody in charge, or anything of a medical nature. I went down to what is now the public pool. It was rather simple in those days. I came here for a month and I improved so much that I came back the following spring. But people had heard about it.

"One day . . . a messenger came up the hill to Mr.

Loyless and said, 'Two people have been carried off the train down at the station. What shall we do with them? Neither of them can walk.'

"Well, we held a consultation. . . . We did not know what to do with them so I sent for Dr. Johnson. He came and looked them over and guaranteed that they did not have heart trouble or something from which they would suddenly die. . . . And then I undertook to be doctor and physiotherapist all rolled into one. I taught Fred Botts to swim. I taught them all at least to play around in the water. I remember there were two quite large ladies. And when I was trying to teach them an exercise which I had really invented, which was the elevating exercise in the medium of water, one of these ladies found great difficulty in getting both feet down to the bottom of the pool. Well, I would take one large knee and I would force this large knee and leg down until the foot rested firmly on the bottom. And then I would say, 'Have you got it?' and she would say, 'Yes,' and I would say, 'Hold it, hold it.' Then I would reach up and get hold of the other knee very quickly and start to put it down and the number-one knee would pop up. This used to go on for half an hour at a time. But before I left in the spring, I could get both those knees down at the same time.

"I called that my medical practice, the first and last time that I have ever practiced medicine and physiotherapy. After I get through at the White House, I hope the medical fraternity will allow me to come back and practice here. I feel I would be rather good at giving exercises in the water. At least, I have had more exercise in the water, over a longer period of time, than anybody else in captivity in this country. . . ."

The procession turned into the driveway of Georgia Hall. A few of the President's friends let go and unashamedly sobbed. From the crowd there lifted the drawn strains of an accordion. The cortege stopped. Graham Jackson, who had missed his chance to entertain the President the evening before, stepped from behind a column and played "Going Home." As he played, Jackson's dark face was a distillation of painful, unbelieving, everlasting regret.

Then the drums resumed their awful, muffled beating and the cortege moved on. Thirty-six minutes after it had left the Little White House, the procession arrived at the railroad station in the village. There another crowd waited. Ten military pallbearers assisted by three undertakers lifted the casket up the trainside ramp. The burden weighed almost eight hundred pounds. A long window of the railroad car had been removed. They handed the casket through the window to ten servicemen inside, who laid it on the pine bier. The carpenter had done his work well; just a few inches of the top of the flag-draped coffin could be seen through the window. A guard of four servicemen—Army, Navy, Marine, and Coast Guard—posted itself at each corner of the coffin, standing like stone statues.

Patterson, the undertaker, searched the bare car for a place to hide the gadgetry and chemicals for sealing the casket. They would be needed by the funeral director who was to take over in Washington. He shoved them under the bier where the Marine blankets would hide them. A Secret Service man, ever suspicious, stopped him and made Patterson explain in detail what he was up to. Finally, the Secret Service man gave in.

Hardly anyone noticed the moment the train began to move. The track to Atlanta slopes downward at about a one-degree grade. The engineer let the train glide down the slope, touching his throttle ever so slightly. The smokestack never chugged until the train was out of the station.

It was as though the President had slipped away on smooth glass from the village he loved.

At Georgia Hall, Graham Jackson found himself seized by an overpowering desire to play the piano. He went to the recreation hall.

"I began playing light music, nothing bouncy, but nothing too sad either," Jackson recalls. "One by one, the patients wheeled in. They just sat, didn't talk. They must have wanted music too, because they stayed. Then I began hearing old F.D.R.'s voice, just like when people would fuss around him at dinner. 'Go on now,' he'd say, 'don't bother with me, take care of the patients.' I could just see that big head of his rear back so noble and go, 'Ha, ha, ha,' in that big round way of his, 'Ha, ha, ha. Go on now and see that all the patients are happy.' I changed the kind of music I was playing. I began things like 'Five Feet Two, Eyes of Blue.' I felt the cheer coming back to the room, just like he'd want. I never stopped playing till eight-thirty that night. I don't think anybody went to eat all day."

13 "And the Government Still Lives"

On the morning they came to carry Franklin D. Roosevelt away from Warm Springs, Harry S. Truman awoke in Washington at six-thirty with an urgent, dreamlike recollection that some extraordinary thing had happened to him—and was calling him to wakefulness. Then he remembered he was now President of the United States, and he bounded out of bed.

Hugh Fulton came to the Truman apartment for breakfast. Fulton, a young ex-Wall Street lawyer, had been the chief counsel of Truman's Senate committee.

When the two men left for the President's car a few minutes before nine, several reporters waiting on the sidewalk speculated that Fulton would become the new Attorney General. (As it turned out, he did not.) One of the waiting reporters was Ernest B. Vaccaro, of the Associated Press Senate staff, who had traveled with Truman during his Vice-Presidential campaign. By a single gesture, the new President quickly dramatized that a new personality was moving into the seat of power, that the whole tone of government in America was about to experience an astonishing change.

"Hey, Tony," the Chief Executive called, "if you're going down to the White House, you may as well hop in with me."

The other reporters, attuned to watching a President move, even in a motor car, with a distant grandeur, blinked.

In the car, the President talked in what Vaccaro has described as "quiet, almost prayerful tones." He said: "There have been few men in all history the equal of the man into whose shoes I am stepping today. I pray God I can measure up to the task. I know that I am ready to give all that I have. . . . I will need the support of the best patriotism and brains of our country. I have no doubt but that I'll get it.

"I just want the folks I love to know that if we can't get together in the old informal way, it is not of my choosing. Tell them that, will you? You know, if I could have my way, I'd have them all come in without knocking.

"You know how it will be. My schedule will be a busy one every day. It will be crowded with official appointments. I'll have all I can do to see everyone I must see in the course of these duties."

Vaccaro asked when the Truman family expected to move into the White House.

The President said: "I want Mrs. Roosevelt to stay just as long as she will. I'm comfortable where I am."

As the car drew up to the White House, Bill Simmons, the chief receptionist, greeted the new President at the door of the Executive Wing.

"People were running around like wild," Simmons says. "Calls were coming from everywhere. Everybody wanted to be one of the first to see him. I asked Mr. Truman when

Matt Connelly, his confidential secretary on the Hill, was coming in. He said Connelly had to hold the fort at the Capitol for a few days. Then he asked me, 'You know what to do, don't you?' I said, 'Yes sir.' He said, 'Then go out there and handle things till Matt gets here.' Suddenly I was the President's appointment secretary."

With the eye of an historian as well as a participant, Jonathan Daniels observed the morning's drama: "Truman tried to keep his appointment list, on the first day in the Presidency, restricted to the men close to the tremendous military and diplomatic jobs. . . . But there were both pressure and confusion in the White House lobby. Some of the old authority was relaxed; new authority was assumed sometimes without right. There was tug and pull for place even among those who guarded the security of the President. Some people got in who looked and acted less like mourners than looters."

Secretary of State Stettinius was first to see Truman. He said that his department each day prepared a two-page summary of diplomatic developments for the President's attention. The President then asked Stettinius to produce a brief outline of the status of American foreign relations. The memorandum, which reached Mr. Truman later in the day, was in effect a digest of the final problems that had troubled the mind of Franklin Roosevelt:

> UNITED KINGDOM. Mr. Churchill's policy is based fundamentally upon cooperation with the United States. It is based secondarily on maintaining the unity of the three great powers but the British Government has been showing increasing apprehension of Russia and her intentions. . . .
>
> SOVIET UNION. Since the Yalta Conference the Soviet Government has taken a firm and uncompromising position on nearly every major question that has arisen in our relations. The more important of these are the Polish question, the application of the Crimea agreement on liberated areas, the

agreement of the exchange of liberated prisoners of war and civilians, and the San Francisco Conference. . . .

POLAND. The present situation relating to Poland is highly unsatisfactory with the Soviet authorities consistently sabotaging Ambassador Harriman's efforts in the Moscow Commission to hasten the implementation of the decisions at the Crimea Conference. Direct appeals to Marshal Stalin have not yet produced any worthwhile results. . . .

GERMANY. . . . Agreements have been reached with the United Kingdom and the Soviet Union on the text of the instrument of unconditional surrender, on control machinery for Germany, and on zones of occupation. . . .

SUPPLIES FOR LIBERATED AREAS. A problem of urgent importance to the U.S. is that of supplies for areas liberated from enemy occupation. The chaos and collapse which may result in these countries from starvation, unemployment and inflation can be averted principally by making available essential civilian supplies. Political stability and the maintenance of democratic governments which can withstand the pressures of extremist groups depend on the restoration of a minimum of economic stability. It is essential that we organize ourselves at once to meet this problem.

Of all these, the Polish question was the most pressing. The controversy revolved around three alternatives. The United States and Great Britain had recognized a Polish government-in-exile, which was functioning in London. This group, however, had opposed the march of the Red Army through Poland, and it was plain that the Russians, who now occupied Poland, would not accept its establishment. As an alternative, Stalin had proposed a group known as the Lublin government, which he maintained was the de facto government. He claimed it was truly Polish in origin and policy and had popular support. In the eyes of the American and British governments, however, it was purely subservient to the Soviets. At Yalta, Roosevelt, Churchill, and Stalin had agreed on a compromise. The

Lublin government was to be expanded by including certain democratic leaders then in Poland and others living abroad. As soon as possible this government was to hold a free, unfettered election based on universal suffrage and secret ballot. There were to be candidates of all anti-Nazi parties in Poland. The Russians, after agreeing to this plan, were failing now to carry through on it. On this question, it was becoming clear, the one world envisioned after the San Francisco conference could be cracked in two.

Shortly after Stettinius departed, Secretary of War Stimson, Secretary of the Navy Forrestal, and the Chief of Staff to the President, Admiral William D. Leahy, entered the oval office. They were followed by the staff chiefs of each of the services: General George C. Marshall, Admiral Ernest J. King, and Air Force Lieutenant General Barney M. Giles.

Their summary was brief: Germany would not be defeated for at least six months (the unconditional surrender, as it turned out, was signed twenty-five days later); and Japan would not be vanquished for a year and a half (Japan surrendered in four months).

As his first morning in office approached its end, Harry Truman demonstrated once again that his government was to have an individual, even surprising, tone. Having an urgent matter to discuss with leaders of Congress, he invited them to a one o'clock luncheon. But instead of calling them to the White House, he offered to meet them at the Capitol; and instead of timing a grand Presidential entrance at the appointed hour, he breezed in a half hour early. In the office of Leslie Biffle, the Secretary of the Senate Majority, he waited; the Senate was still in session.

Majority Leader Barkley, Senator Wallace White of Maine, and Senator Robert F. Wagner of New York had already spoken words of tribute and grief for the departed leader. Now Senator Arthur H. Vandenberg of Michigan had the floor.

"Mr. President, words are pathetic messengers," he said. "When the country staggered eighty years ago under the awful impact of the news that Abraham Lincoln was dead, James A. Garfield concluded a message to the Nation with the ringing words, which I now make my own, 'God reigns, and the Government in Washington still lives.' "

At twelve-forty the Senate recessed and there was a rush by thirteen leaders of the Senate and four of the House for Biffle's office. Truman told them he thought it would be a good idea for him to address a joint session of Congress. It would not be fitting to do so, he said, before the burial of Roosevelt, but he wanted no time lost after that. He suggested Monday, April 16th—only three days away.

Truman asked each of his listeners what he thought of the idea. Most of them readily agreed; a few were opposed or doubtful. But Truman said he felt a need to emphasize his support for the policies of Roosevelt and to ask for continued bipartisan coöperation in the conduct of the war. Finally, the minority agreed.

"Harry," said one of the original doubters, "you were planning to come whether we liked it or not."

"You know I would have," said Truman, "but I would rather do it with your full and understanding support and welcome."

When the meeting ended, Biffle opened his office doors. A crowd of Senate employees waiting outside filed in. Senate page boys formed in a long white-shirted line. The President shook the hand of each. In an adjoining room, Capitol newspapermen waited to catch a word from him. Truman went in to greet them.

"Boys, if newspapermen ever pray," he said, "pray for me now. I don't know whether you fellows ever had a load of hay fall on you, but when they told me yesterday what had happened, I felt like the moon, the stars, and all the planets had fallen on me. I've got the most terribly responsible job a man ever had."

A reporter said, "Good luck, Mr. President."

Truman shook his head wistfully and said, "I wish you didn't have to call me that."

A page boy, sixteen-year-old John Bunch of Statesville, North Carolina, asked Truman for an autograph. The President gave the boy his signature, and remarked, "This is the boy that remembered me when I was in trouble." Later the boy explained that there had been a few days interval between Truman's resignation as a Senator and his inauguration as Vice-President. "He was out of a job," John explained sheepishly, "so I asked him if he'd like to come to work for me."

Truman headed for the stairs, hesitated, and walked to the door of the Senate cloakroom. He stood there and gazed. Then he walked through the cloakroom and opened a door to the Senate Chamber. Again, he looked. Twenty-four hours earlier he had presided here over a debate on a Mexican water treaty.

A group of page boys stood up. One of them said, "We're going to miss you, Mr. President."

"I'm going to miss you, too," the President replied.

Then he entered the Vice-President's office adjoining the cloakroom, greeted the staff, and led his Secret Service escort in a dash down the steps of the Capitol.

There was something peculiar—incongruous—about the dash down the stairs. It seemed odd, after so many years, to see a President of the United States walking.

Truman had an appointment at the White House at two-thirty with a man who was perhaps more anxious to see the new President than he cared to show. Five days earlier, James F. Byrnes had left the Roosevelt Administration, saying that he needed a rest. But now, on little more than a moment's notice, Byrnes had flown to Washington in the plane offered by Forrestal to confer with his old friend, Harry Truman.

"I had known Byrnes well for years," Truman recalls, "and I wanted to get his firsthand account of what had gone on at Yalta, and all the information he had of the meetings between Roosevelt, Churchill, and Stalin. I had heard that he had personally made shorthand notes of all the secret meetings he had attended. I greeted him as an old friend when he entered, and we talked for half an hour about everything he could recall without referring to his notes. Then I asked him to transcribe his notes for me. During our discussion I had told Byrnes that I was considering asking him to become Secretary of State after the San Francisco conference. In considering Byrnes for this most important Cabinet post, a number of factors influenced me. The first of these was the question of succession to the presidency. Under the law, as matters now stood, the next man in line after me was the Secretary of State. Byrnes had felt that by virtue of his record of service to the party and the country he had been the logical choice to be the running mate of Franklin Roosevelt in the 1944 election. In fact, he had asked me to nominate him and give him my support before that convention.

"As it turned out, Roosevelt and the convention willed otherwise, and Byrnes, undoubtedly, was deeply disappointed and hurt. I thought that my calling on him at this time might help balance things up."

That evening, President Truman, weary and laden with documents to read, headed for 4701 Connecticut Avenue— an executive, like many others, returning home after a hard day at the office; except that his closed car was followed by a long, open one with Secret Service men riding the running board.

"I couldn't help feeling uncomfortable," Truman has said. "There was no escaping the fact that my privacy and personal freedom were to be greatly restricted from now on. I even began to realize, as I rode toward my apartment that evening, that our neighbors were beginning to be imposed upon. They were no longer able to come and go as they pleased. To enter their own homes it was now necessary for them to be properly identified and cleared by the Secret Service men.

"They were all very nice about it, but Mrs. Truman and I felt that the sooner we could move to an official residence the easier it would be."

One of the people inconvenienced—although Mr. Truman didn't know it—was his apartment house switchboard operator. The realization had spread in Washington—where during the war, government people were desperate for housing—that an apartment was about to be vacated, and a good one: two bedrooms, foyer, large living room, dining room, kitchen, and bath, at a rent-controlled cost of $120 a month. All day the switchboard operator was harassed by calls from prospective tenants. She developed a stock answer: "The owner has asked me to save this apartment for at least three different people. But I will be happy to keep you in mind."

14

"A Very Wretched Day"

On the morning of Friday the 13th many people besides Harry S. Truman awoke with a sleepy knowledge that there was something special to remember. As they blinked themselves awake and remembered—*President Roosevelt —dead*—some felt the tipsy aura of morning after; the queasy, tense, oppressive hints of a hangover.

Peculiar things happened that day, one after another. It was as though the globe itself had rolled out of bed from the wrong side.

In New York, an odd series of rumors had begun to spread. One concerned Van Johnson, the movie star; another, Jack Dempsey. Both were rumored to be dead. Before long these rumors merged into a report that Johnson and Dempsey had been killed together.

Each hour brought new "victims." Mayor La Guardia was high on the list of those reported dead; so were Harry Hopkins, former Governor Herbert H. Lehman, Charlie Chaplin, Frank Sinatra, Al Jolson, Errol Flynn, Babe Ruth,

Jack Benny, and former New York Mayor Jimmy Walker. Mostly they were reported to have perished alone, but sometimes in tandem.

The New York *Times*, which tallies its incoming calls according to type, in a single hour handled 10,498 inquiries counted as "rumor or frivolous." Swamped operators pressed their callers for the sources of the rumors. People were vague. "Oh, it's going around." "There are lots of rumors in our building." *Where? Who told you?* "Oh, up here, all around Thirtieth Street." "A friend in a drug store told me. Is it true or not?"

The New York Telephone Company registered a volume of calls that kept pace with Thursday's, when the usual daily rate had been exceeded by a million. Calls to substantiate rumors poured into banks, government offices, even corner drug stores. Curiously, many such calls came to the New York headquarters of the Office of Price Administration; this agency, which enforced rent control and issued ration stamps for food and gasoline, was in the minds of many the embodiment of supreme authority.

Investigation finally explained the Jack Dempsey rumor. In a door of the famous restaurant bearing his name at Broadway and 49th Street, a sign was discovered: CLOSED ON ACCOUNT OF DEATH OF OUR BELOVED PRESIDENT, JACK DEMPSEY RESTAURANT CORP. The last two words, however, had been obscured by the doorframe. But the other rumors remained unexplained.

Other curious repercussions of the President's death came from unexpected directions. The War Production Board warned Mayor La Guardia, as president of the United States Conference of Mayors, that a run on dark fabrics for mourning could be disastrous to the nation's civilian cotton supply. La Guardia, in turn, implored other mayors not to drape black cloth on public buildings.

Many citizens, owning flags but no flagpoles, hung their

flags upside down outside their windows. This horrified a public relations officer of the Navy. He asked radio stations to announce that such flags, to indicate mourning, should be hung right side up with a black crepe bowknot at each corner. A flag displayed upside down, he hastened to point out, was not a sign of mourning but a signal of distress.

The United Feature Syndicate informed its subscribing papers that Eleanor Roosevelt's column, "My Day," would not appear this day. The reason it gave was that the author had failed to submit her copy.

The New York Stock Exchange opened with a two-minute period of prayer. There were fears that the national shock would cause a sell-off. But confidence reigned. In all, 1,803,900 shares were traded, the largest volume in more than a month; utilities hit a 1945 peak.

Near Times Square, a man displayed a board full of old F.D.R. campaign buttons newly trimmed with black ribbons. "Hey," he shouted, "get-cher Roosevelt memorial buttons, fit-teen cents." People drove him off the streets.

In the teeming garment district, workers and bosses together left their shops at three P.M. and massed, twenty thousand strong, in Seventh Avenue between 28th and 29th Streets, normally one of the most boisterous streets in the world. There they stood, in complete silence, as Cantor M.S. Yardeini chanted the ancient Hebrew prayer for the dead, "El Mole Rachmim."

In Washington, Philip Murray, president of the C.I.O., called upon all union members to commemorate F.D.R. by staying on the job where they were needed. But in Madison, Wisconsin, eight hundred C.I.O. steel workers at the Gisholt Machine Company walked off their jobs. Their grievance was that the company was not flying a flag to honor the dead President. The company replied that it was raining, so the colors should not be raised.

While the war plant stood paralyzed, a labor-management committee called Truax Field for arbitration of the dispute. An Air Force authority ruled that under the circumstances a half-masted flag could fly. The flag was raised and production resumed.

Near London, England, a morning suburban railroad coach rattled into the city, rocking a silent crowd of commuters. They read their papers and read them again. One rider was weeping. A gray-haired man arose in the aisle, his newspaper to his chest. The others looked up. The elderly man began to address his fellows: "Mr. Roosevelt was a gentleman in every sense of the word. He was faithful to the trust placed in him by the people of the United States and faithful to the cause of mankind the world over." He looked around, as though for additional words; finding none, he slowly sat down.

At Buckingham Palace, the *Court Circular*, a daily chronicle of the affairs of the royal household, for the first time in its history reported the death of a head of state who was not related to the British ruling family.

In Central Hall, opposite Westminster Abbey, the Reverend William E. Sangster heard a tap-tapping down the corridor, the cane of ninety-six-year-old Reverend Scott Liggett. Sangster greeted the older man and said, "This is a very wretched day."

"Indeed," said the aged clergyman. "I haven't heard such distressing news since the day President Lincoln was shot." At the time of the earlier calamity, Liggett was sixteen years old.

The London bureau of the U.S. Office of War Information received an urgent call from Madame Tussaud's wax museum in Baker Street. They needed a list of measurements of the new American President—height, weight, collar size, shoe size, even a photograph of the back of Mr. Truman's head. Victor Weybright, an O.W.I. official, cabled Washington and even he was surprised when, two hours later, all the information was cabled back; all, that is, except the rear photograph which took two days longer.

In the House of Commons the galleries were filled at eleven A.M. Prime Minister Churchill entered the chamber with Anthony Eden, who was about to leave for the funeral in Washington. All the members of the Government wore black ties.

"The House will have heard with the deepest sorrow," Churchill began, his voice shaking noticeably, his enunciation less distinct than usual, "the grievous news which has come to us from across the Atlantic"—his speech faltered —"which conveys to us the loss of the famous President of the United States whose friendship for the cause of freedom and for the cause of the weak and the poor"—here his voice clearly broke—"have won him immortal fame. It is not fitting that we should continue our work this day. I feel that the House will wish to render its token of respect to the memory of this great departed statesman and war leader by adjourning immediately."

Moscow newspapers did something extraordinary—in fact, unprecedented. They printed Roosevelt's picture and the news of his death on the first page. In Russian papers, foreign news always appears on the back pages. This custom had not been broken even to announce the attack on Pearl Harbor or the opening of the second front. C. L. Sulzberger of the New York *Times* cabled his newspaper from Moscow: "It may seem strange to Americans that many, many people here who never even saw Mr. Roosevelt with their own eyes have wept and are weeping over what they feel is a personal tragedy. This bereavement has apparently brought the Soviet and the American people psychologically closer at this moment than at any time in the personal knowledge of this correspondent."

Late in the day, Ambassador Harriman called on Marshal Stalin. The Soviet leader was subdued, visibly moved. He described Roosevelt as the welding force in the great alliance. Then he asked what he could do to insure that the solidarity would be maintained. Harriman seized the opening. He said the best thing the Soviet government could do to protect the alliance would be to send its highest-ranking foreign affairs official, Foreign Minister Molotov, to the San Francisco conference. Molotov, sitting beside Stalin, said that there were other important things he needed to attend to. Harriman replied that nothing was more important than the success and prestige of the conference. Stalin asked how Molotov could get there in time; the Soviets had no long-range planes available. Harriman immediately offered to furnish one. After a pause, Stalin agreed. Harriman hurried back to the embassy to radio Secretary Stettinius—who brought the news immediately to President Truman.

Somewhere in the Pacific, not too far from Okinawa, the aircraft carrier *Hornet* was cruising. Standing watch on the flag bridge, Lieutenant John Roosevelt, U.S.N.R., was keeping radio contact with other ships in the fleet. One of them called the *Hornet*'s code. It identified itself by voice code as the *Ulvert M. Moore*, a ship under the command of Lieutenant Commander Franklin D. Roosevelt, Jr. The voice had a familiar Harvard-Groton turn. The two voices exchanged a few syllables to corroborate the recognition, using no names.

Then the voice from the *Ulvert M. Moore* asked: "Are you making it home, Old Man?"

"No," replied the *Hornet*. "Are you?"

"Nope. Let's clean it up out here first. So long, Old Man—over."

"So long—out."

At Warm Springs, Georgia, a heavy wooden ramp that had been built hastily by the Marines for lifting the President's casket from the hearse to the railroad car was torn to pieces by souvenir hunters soon after the funeral train disappeared around the first bend of the tracks.

15

"The Lonesome Train"

The funeral train clicked slowly along the rails across the sun-baked green flatlands of middle Georgia. President Roosevelt always liked to ride the rails slowly. From Washington to Warm Springs a fortnight earlier, the train had lazed along at a top speed of thirty miles an hour. The trip had taken twenty-two-and-a-half-hours, when it could have been made in a single circling of the clock.

Now Steve Early instructed the engineer that there was no need to pour on the coal. A twenty-four-hour trip would bring the party to Washington soon enough. Perhaps there would be people along the route who had come to watch the train go by.

Early gave each of the press association reporters, Smith, Oliver, and Nixon, a copy of the Jefferson Day speech the President was to have delivered that night. It had been drafted by a ghost writer employed by the Democratic National Committee, redrafted by Robert Sherwood, redrafted again by Jonathan Daniels. Roosevelt finally had used parts of all three. The ghost writer's ending had said: "The only limit to our realization of tomorrow will be our doubt of today." Roosevelt liked that. But he crossed out "doubt of today" and, with an unsteady hand, wrote, "doubts of today." Then he added a sentence, his last words to the people of the United States:

"Let us move forward with strong and active faith."

The reporters, too exhausted from their night-long outpouring of words to feel their own weariness, plunged like dutiful machines into stories about the speech. They would dispatch their stories when the train arrived at Atlanta.

In the *Ferdinand Magellan*, the President's lounge and bedroom car, Mrs. Roosevelt applied her mind not to mourning but to duty. Late in the morning she sent for Grace Tully. The two women worked out a card to acknowledge the dozens of condolence messages that had come by wire to Warm Springs and that now were piling up by the thousands in Washington. (One of the messages, from a little boy in Chicago—it was accompanied by a bouquet picked from his back yard—said, "I was sorry I couldn't come to the funeral.") The card they devised was to have a thin black border and read:

Mrs. Roosevelt and her family
thank you very much for your condolences
and appreciate your kind thought

Then Mrs. Roosevelt turned to her husband's secretary and hesitantly asked: "Did Franklin ever give you any instructions about his burial?"

Miss Tully recalls: "She had difficulty saying that. Her eyes welled and her voice broke. It was only momentary. It was the only time during the whole ordeal that I ever saw her almost lose her control."

Miss Tully was not able to provide a useful answer. Almost a year earlier, during an afternoon mail session when the President and his secretary had paused for a moment of personal conversation, he had said: "Grace, if anything should happen to me while I am at sea, I want to be buried at sea. You know it has always seemed like home to me."

Miss Tully had replied that that was one wish she hoped would not be carried out. "I personally do not like it or even the thought of it," she told him, "and I believe the people of the country would feel as I do."

A few months later Miss Tully was lunching with the President and Miss Suckley when he asked: "What ever happened to a memorandum I dictated about my burial arrangements? Do you know where it is?"

Miss Tully said she knew nothing about it, but that she was certain it had not been dictated to her. She did, however, order a search of the files, but it produced nothing. The President said: "If you can't locate it, remind me to dictate another."

He never did. (Three days after the President was buried, such a memorandum, dated December 26, 1937, was found in his bedroom safe at the White House. It had not been dictated, but was written by him in pencil and addressed to his oldest son, James.)*

One thing of which Mrs. Roosevelt felt sure was that her husband did not wish to lie in state. "We have talked often," she has said, "when there had been a funeral at the Capitol in which a man had lain in state and the crowds had gone by the open coffin, of how much we disliked the practice; and we had made up our minds that we would never allow it." She also felt sure, even before her talk with Miss Tully in the railroad car, that somewhere, sometime, her husband had faced up to the unpleasant practicality of determining his wishes and preparing them for his survivors.

* The text of this memorandum appears in the appendix.

"He was too historically minded to do otherwise," Mrs. Roosevelt says. "I would be unconcerned about such things and he would get angry. He would say, 'It's important how things will appear in history.' This is something he inherited from his mother. She was very concerned with history. That's why she always collected every snitch of everything and kept them as family mementoes."

When Miss Tully left, Mrs. Roosevelt remained alone for most of the long, somber ride to Washington. No one knows whether the widow maintained in privacy her stoic composure. But fifteen years later, she permitted herself to talk about her memories of that day: "At a time like that, you don't really feel your own feelings. When you're in a position of being caught in a pageant, you become part of a world outside yourself and you act almost like an automaton. You recede as a person. You build a façade for everyone to see and you live separately inside the façade. Something comes to protect you.

"I was well prepared for it. My grandmother brought me up to prepare for it, in a social way. I was never permitted as a child to say that I had a headache. I was trained to put personal things in the background. It was a good preparation for the disciplines of public life, especially for life in the White House.

"I recall one night we had a big reception at the White House. I was just as ill as I could be. I went upstairs, became sick, and came down again. This happened a second and a third time. But it never occurred to me to leave the party before it was over and go to bed.

"In the autumn of 1941, my brother died at Walter Reed Hospital. But I had to put it in the background because things had to go on.

"We know that death is inevitable. You have to be able to bear the inevitable. You're not given any other choice."

As the train rolled into the city of Atlanta, threading its way between factories, squalid garages, and the dwellings of the poor, immense clusters of people at every crossing stood awed, hushed. Near the terminal, traffic jammed for blocks. As the train passed under the Mitchell Street viaduct, a streetcar passing overhead stopped. Passengers stood up to watch.

Atlanta. One day Franklin Roosevelt came to town, and the people of Atlanta filled their ball park to listen. It was 1935; everyone was in trouble. He spoke plainly:

"I can realize that gentlemen in well-warmed and well-stocked clubs will discourse on the expenses of Government and the suffering that they are going through because their Government is spending money for work relief. I wish I could take some of these men out on the battle-line of human necessity, and show them the facts that we in the Government are facing. Some of these same gentlemen tell me that a dole would be more economical than work relief. That is true. But the men who tell me that have, unfortunately, too little contact with the true America to realize that in this business of relief we are dealing with properly self-respecting Americans to whom a mere dole outrages every instinct of individual independence. Most Americans want to give something for what they get. That something, which in this case is honest work, is the saving barrier between them and moral disintegration. I propose to build that barrier high and keep it high."

Track 9 was fenced by two companies of white-gloved soldiers from Camp Sibert, Alabama, bearing bayoneted rifles at present arms. Only a few dozen newspaper and radio reporters and local dignitaries had been permitted on the platform. They gathered at the last car, which bore the flag-draped coffin.

Steve Early stepped from the car, and Mayor William
B. Hartsfield handed him a basket of white gladioli and red
roses. The two men stepped inside and placed them near
the President's head. They were the only flowers in the
car. Mayor Hartsfield removed one rose from the spray,
returned to the platform, and handed it to Mrs. Charles F.
Palmer, the wife of a New Deal housing official.

Hartsfield and Early entered the *Ferdinand Magellan*
where the Mayor said to Mrs. Roosevelt: "There are no
words to express our feelings of sorrow today."

"I understand," she replied.

Prettyman, the valet, was walking Fala along the platform. The dog's tail wagged busily as flash bulbs went off.
Workmen replenished the train's ice supply, a new crew
assumed command, and at 2:10 P.M., forty minutes after
it had arrived, the train resumed its journey toward the
nation's capital.

Overhead, small private planes circled the train. In the
dining car, the three press correspondents sat, too tense to
attempt sleep, too tired to talk. They were nearing Gainesville, Georgia. Suddenly, Merriman Smith's arm pointed to
a cotton field they were passing. In the middle of the field,
a portly Negro woman, fallen to her knees, flailed her
hands in the air. Other Negro women nearby fell to the
ground, clasping their hands together. They were sharecroppers at spring planting, in a posture of total sup-
plication.

Gainesville, Georgia. On March 23, 1938, the President
had come here and described conditions by a word many
in the crowd had never heard. He spoke of feudalism.

*"When you come down to it, there is little difference
between the feudal system and the Fascist system. If you
believe in the one, you lean to the other.*

"With the overwhelming majority of the people of this

State, I oppose feudalism. So do many among those who by virtue of their circumstances in life belong to the most prosperous five per cent of the population . . . they are coming more. and more to see that the continuation of the American system calls for the elimination of special privilege, the dissemination of the whole of the truth, and participation in prosperity by the people at the bottom of the ladder, as well as those. in the middle and at the top.

"One thing is certain—we are not going back to the old days. We are going forward to better days. . . ."

The afternoon sun dimmed, then dipped. At the edge of darkness, the train chugged through a new crowd at Greenville, South Carolina. Here a new railroad crew, like runners in a relay, took command. Before stepping into his cab, the engineer fastened an American flag across the front of his engine.

At 10:45 P.M., late for a quiet Southern town, the train came to Charlotte, North Carolina. Flanking the station for five solid blocks, people huddled together in the dark. As the train halted, a boy scout troop began to sing "Onward, Christian Soldiers."

"It started ragged at first, but then it spread and swelled," Merriman Smith recalls. "Soon eight or ten thousand voices were singing like an organ. Those people were scared to death. They weren't singing for a departed soul. They were singing for themselves, to hold themselves up, as though they were asking, 'What are we going to do now?'"

Harold Oliver adds: "When the hymn ended, Negroes knelt down and began to sing spirituals. A lot of the whites joined them. The Negroes were separated to one side, by themselves. Most of them never got to vote for F.D.R., but they came out late at night to pray for him."

North Carolina. On August 18, 1937, Roosevelt had
come here and spoken out as men of politics seldom speak
in the South.

*"They tell you that America drifts toward the Scylla of
dictatorship on the one hand, or the Charybdis of anarchy
on the other. Their anchor for the salvation of the Ship of
State is Macaulay's anchor: 'Supreme power in the hands
of a class, numerous indeed, but select; of an educated
class, of a class which is, and knows itself to be, deeply
interested in the security of property and the maintenance
of order.'*

*"Mine is a different anchor. They do not believe in
democracy—I do. My anchor is democracy—and more
democracy. And, my friends, I am of the firm belief
that the Nation, by an overwhelming majority, supports
my opposition to the vesting of supreme power in the hands
of any class, numerous but select."*

Now in the darkness, its shades drawn, the train was a
streak of black cutting through the moonlit countryside.
That is, all the cars were black except one: the dimly lit
rear coach, with its visible fragment of a flag and four
stone-still sentries. The car shone by contrast with a
peculiar brilliance, as it slid by the solemn crowds.

Twice in the late hours, Lizzie McDuffie walked through
the train to the *Ferdinand Magellan*. Mrs. Roosevelt had not
brought a maid with her and Lizzie offered to help. Each
time, Mrs. Roosevelt thanked her and said there was nothing
she needed. Toward midnight Lizzie went to bed.

"I don't think I slept hardly any that night," she recalls.
"I turned off my lights and lifted my shade. I thought
about everything in the world, about all the trips we'd
made to Warm Springs, to California with the grand-
children, and different places like that. Lying in my berth,

and knowing the President's body was lying in the back, I couldn't get away from thinking of conditions of things when Mr. Roosevelt became President. I lay there and thought about the bread lines I saw on the very day I was leaving my home in Atlanta to go to Washington to work for him. I thought about a man who was a friend of ours, who was an insurance collector who was very prosperous. He had lost his position because people didn't have any money to pay their life insurance. I thought of him so much because three years later I remember going home and meeting him on the street all dressed up nice. He had gotten his job back collecting insurance and his children had started back to school. It was just another picture than what it was when I left.

"And I lay there and thought of the terrible blunder I made when the King and Queen of England came to Washington. There was a man named Charlie Thompson that worked at the White House and he wanted their autograph. One day I overheard him tell somebody, 'Take this picture upstairs and see if you can't get Lizzie McDuffie to get them to autograph it. Lizzie'll do anything you ask her for.' Well, I heard that and spoke up. I said, 'I'll ask. They can't do anything except say yes or no.' And I asked one of those English people to try to get it for me. Later Mrs. Roosevelt said to me, 'Why, Mrs. McDuffie'—most of the time that's what she called me— 'why, you shouldn't have asked any member of the Queen's staff. You should have carried it to Mrs. Helm or Miss Thompson.' She wasn't angry, though. Mrs. Roosevelt never got angry. She'd just say, 'There's one thing about it, Lizzie. If you benefit by the mistake you have made, then everything will be all right.' She is the most considerate person that was ever born, Mrs. Roosevelt is."

In the *Ferdinand Magellan*, Mrs. Roosevelt was thinking other thoughts:

"I lay in my berth all night with the window shade up, looking out at the countryside he had loved and watching the faces of the people at stations, and even at the cross-roads, who came to pay their last tribute all through the night.

"The only recollection I clearly have is thinking about 'The Lonesome Train,' the musical poem about Lincoln's death." (*A lonesome train on a lonesome track/ Seven coaches painted black / A slow train, a quiet train / Carrying Lincoln home again . . .*) "I had always liked it so well —and now this was so much like it.

"I was truly surprised by the people along the way; not only at the stops, but at every crossing. I didn't expect that because I hadn't thought a thing about it.

"I never realized the full scope of the devotion to him until after he died—until that night and after. Later, I couldn't go into a subway in New York or a cab without people stopping me to say they missed the way the President used to talk to them. They'd say 'He used to talk to me about my government.'

"There was a real dialogue between Franklin and the people. He would read samplings of his mail and I always prepared small piles of my letters for him. He always knew what the reaction was to what he was doing, and he could respond to the reaction. That dialogue seems to have disappeared from the government since he died."

Forward in the train, Bill Hassett, as he always did when he was away from Washington with the President, made a few notes in his diary before retiring. On this night he wrote:

"F.D.R. made his last journey from Warm Springs this morning—the strangeness and unreality of all that has happened in so brief a time. President Truman has already taken over and is, I suppose, at the desk in the Executive Office where the late Boss sat for more than twelve years.

The deeper lesson of it is that no matter how unexpected the change, the succession is quiet and orderly and the processes of government continue."

The passengers passed the night fitfully; the train moved through town after town, the crowds in each waiting unfailingly. At 6:20 A.M., the train reached Charlottesville, Virginia. It was coming near now to Washington.

Washington. In the nation's capital, the nation's leader spoke of many things, some to the moment, some to the future and past. Here on Constitution Day, 1937, he spoke of a governmental philosophy.

"The men who wrote the Constitution were the men who fought the Revolution. So when these men planned a new government, they drew the kind of agreement which men make when they really want to work together under it for a very long time. . . .

"For the youngest of nations they drew what is today the oldest written instrument under which men have continuously lived together as a nation. . . .

"The Constitution of the United States was a layman's document, not a lawyer's contract. . . .

"It cost a Civil War to gain recognition of the constitutional power of the Congress to legislate for the territories.

"It cost twenty years of taxation on those least able to pay to recognize the constitutional power of the Congress to levy taxes on those most able to pay.

"It cost twenty years of exploitation of women's labor to recognize the constitutional power of the States to pass minimum wage laws for their protection.

"It has cost twenty years already—and no one knows how many more are to come—to obtain a constitutional interpretation that will let the Nation regulate the ship-

ment in national commerce of goods sweated from the labor of little children.

"We know it takes time to adjust government to the needs of society. But modern history proves that reforms too long delayed or denied have jeopardized peace, undermined democracy and swept away civil and religious liberties. We will no longer be permitted to sacrifice each generation in turn while the law catches up with life."

In the morning, Hassett was given a message that had come overnight from Edith Helm at the White House. Mrs. Helm needed to know Mrs. Roosevelt's preferences as to hymns for the funeral. Mrs. Roosevelt chose "Eternal Father, Strong to Save" and "America."

She added that she wished the service to incorporate the President's words from his first inaugural address, which she believed meant more to him than any of his others:

"The only thing we have to fear is fear itself."

16

"The Average Man"

The people of the United States, waking up on Saturday to their second morning without Roosevelt, were slowly becoming sufficiently clear-eyed to look at a hard, irrevocable fact. Harry S. Truman, whoever he was, was now President of the United States.

But who was he?

The New York *Times* chose the second morning without Roosevelt to offer its readers some cautious reassurance. Its editorial bore a title that seemed to be a contradiction in terms: "President Truman." It said:

"In one of the great moments of history there steps into the office of the Presidency of the United States and into a position of world-wide influence and authority such as no other living American has ever held, a man who is less well known to the people of this country than many other public figures and almost totally unknown abroad. . . . It is . . . part of the longer record of American political life that out of the ranks of the 'practical politicians' and out of the hard, tough schools of the ward machines have come men whose experience in the practical ways of accomplishing sound public purposes made them particularly useful to their country in a time of crisis. . . ."

The darkness surrounding this new figure, through which the *Times* was trying valiantly to whistle, was indeed world-wide. From Paris, the Associated Press reported:

"Perhaps not one Frenchman in ten even knew the new President's name before yesterday. Today it is on everyone's lips."

C. L. Sulzberger wrote from Moscow of "a keen intellectual interest in American politics and in everything concerning President Truman, past, present, and future. This earnest curiosity is exhibited from the very top to the very bottom of the social structure. The Soviet radio has been devoting entire programs to biographical data on the new Chief Executive, whose personality is the subject of even greater conversational interest than the dramatic capture of Vienna."

Tokyo radio, trying to base a comprehensive assessment of the new American leader on a quick interview with a former employee of the Library of Congress, reported that Truman was a hard worker, "who especially exerted his efforts in bettering the conditions of the lower classes," but who was "a little too good-natured" and "not good in politics."

London newspapers were offering American correspondents $150 for a quick thousand words on Truman's career. The Americans were hard put to meet the offer. A London *Mirror* reporter placed a call to Independence, Missouri, and got through to a cousin of Truman, Miss Ethel Noland. The reporter, scratching his imagination, asked how Truman felt about the British. Miss Noland replied with great assurance that Harry felt fine about the

British. In fact, she said, he had visited England in 1917. At that time, she added, he was an artillery officer on his way to Pershing's western front.

In search of enlightenment, an American reporter persuaded Henry P. Chiles, a county employee at Independence, to tell of his early acquaintanceship with Bess Truman, the new First Lady. Mr. Chiles responded:

"She was a great girl. She was the first girl I ever knew who could whistle through her teeth. She could bat a ball as far as any boy in the neighborhood. Now, I don't want you to get the wrong idea about Bess. As she grew up she became very dignified, very popular and well liked."

One man who could size up Truman if he would was Roy Roberts, the managing editor of the Kansas City *Star*. Roberts, on this day, happened to be in Washington. In fact, he was one of the few, outside of top government figures, who had seen the new President during his first day in office.

On America's second day without Roosevelt, Roberts sat down to write about Truman. His article was printed next day in papers across the country:

"Roosevelt was essentially a brilliant patrician . . . which was why he could understand and get on with Churchill, the brilliant Britisher, so well. They were blood brothers, one working the liberal side of the street, the other clinging to conservatism.

"Harry Truman is as far apart from both Roosevelt and Churchill as Hyde Park is from Independence, Mo. The new President is the average man. He has plowed corn—and his mother bragged he plowed a straight row; he sold haberdashery, and failed at it. He worked in a mailing room. He fought bravely in his country's war. Then he started climbing the ladder in politics, with a political machine his sponsor, as the worst handicap to overcome in any possible climb to the Presidency.

"What a story in democracy, that a man approaching 40 and still looking at the rear of a horse as he plowed the corn rows, apparently not a success in life, just a little less than twenty years ago, should find himself today President of the greatest and most powerful nation on earth! The average man who became President in one of the great crises of the world. What a test of democracy if it works. And the sheer fact he is this average man, understands the average man and his quality, is probably Truman's greatest asset as he undertakes these new overpowering responsibilities. . . .

"What sort of man really is Truman?

". . . Scratch under the hide of the new President and you will find not a politician, a statesman, nor a man with overweening ambition, but a country man with deep faiths. The country thinks of Truman as a Kansas Cityian. He isn't. He's a rural Jackson Countyite—down where they really fought the Civil War.

"The offspring of a Confederate veteran, he is really more Southern in viewpoint than Midwestern. A Baptist, once Grand Master of his Masonic Lodge of Missouri, he will think as the average man does, at least outside the big cities. . . . If he develops a weakness, it will be in not always understanding the newly aroused mass consciousness of industrial labor.

"In the Senate Truman's closest friendships were with the Old South. Back home, his closest friendships were with the old Battery B of the 129th Field Artillery, the men with whom he fought in France. It is entirely possible that this feel of the average man may make him a mighty leader for his nation in the years just ahead."

The average man who had become President, always an early riser, arose at dawn on the second day without Roosevelt. Before breakfast he worked over a draft of his

forthcoming speech to Congress. Then he turned to study-
ing a memo from the Secretary of State about the San
Francisco conference. Already there was a disagreement
with Stalin over the three-for-one vote. Stalin was now
insisting that the agreement made by Roosevelt and
Churchill to give membership in the General Assembly to
the Ukraine and White Russia be extended to giving them
seats at the San Francisco conference itself. In behalf of
the United States, the average man who had become President had to decide what to do about it.

The new President arrived at the White House at 8:30.
His first caller was John W. Snyder of St. Louis, a banker
and former official of the Reconstruction Finance Corporation and the Defense Plant Corporation, and an old personal friend. Truman had already decided to appoint
Snyder to an important vacancy, that of Federal Loan
Administrator. After the conference, Truman called Jesse
Jones, the former head of the loan agency, and said that
"the President" had appointed Snyder to the job.

Jones, surprised that he had not been consulted, asked:
"Did he make that appointment before he died?"

"No," Truman answered. "He made it just now."

Truman did not resent the slip. He has commented,
"Everyone, including myself, still continued to think of
Roosevelt as 'the President.' "

The next caller was Henry Morgenthau, Secretary of
the Treasury, Roosevelt's Dutchess County neighbor and
his last official visitor before he died. Morgenthau was glad
to have been summoned by Truman. He wanted to take a
careful, critical look at the new leader, whom he hardly
knew. The conference was surprisingly brief. The average
man who had become President directed the Secretary to
submit as soon as possible a comprehensive report on the
state of the nation's finances, then sent him off.

The next appointment was a peculiar one. It was with

two men: James F. Byrnes, who held no official post, and Henry A. Wallace, the Secretary of Commerce. There was no apparently urgent reason for calling these two together. They conversed circuitously for a few moments, then Truman told the two men he would like them to accompany him to Union Station to meet Roosevelt's funeral train. Whether purposefully or not, they were a brilliantly composed trio: two men whose candidacies for Vice-President had split the Democratic Party, and a third man, the one who got the job. They represented—whether purposefully or not—a trinity of rivals, together at a moment of crisis.

In a closed limousine they rode to the great plaza between Union Station and Capitol Hill. Many thousands were already waiting in the still heat of the morning. At the base of the Christopher Columbus statue, an elderly priest stood alone, eyes closed, lips moving. A formation of Marines, upon a muffled command, saluted as the President's car drove into the station. Hardly anyone in the crowd realized who was in the car.

At 9:50, the funeral train halted in the station. First to enter the last car where the coffin lay was Roosevelt's daughter, Anna, followed by Brigadier General Elliott Roosevelt and his wife, actress Faye Emerson. Elliott had arrived in Washington the day before from England. Then President Truman led the assembled officials into the train.

At 9:58, the funeral procession began. It moved into Delaware Avenue and turned west at Constitution Avenue, a boulevard of rich greenery and proud marble architecture. The route was bordered by a wall of helmeted soldiers, dividing the broad, empty avenue from sidewalks that were overflowing with mourners.

As the cortege appeared, there was first a stunned quiet. Then the heavens thundered fearsomely as a ceiling of twenty-four Army Liberators slid across the sky.

A squadron of motorcycle police led the painfully slow procession. Then came a contingent of armored troops and carriers, followed by truck-borne infantry. The United States Marine Band was next, then a battalion of midshipmen from Annapolis, followed by the United States Navy Band. The two bands, performing alternately, played "Onward, Christian Soldiers," "Adeste Fidelis," the "Dead March" from *Saul*, and Chopin's "Funeral March." After the band came a detachment of service women— WAC's, WAVE's, SPAR's, Women Marines.

Then a black-draped caisson carrying the coffin.

It was so sudden. It came so quietly. It seemed so peculiarly small. Just a big-wheeled wagon, dragged slowly, bearing the flag-covered oblong box. It was not a huge thing at all, as somehow everyone expected it to be. It was small, as though it might be any man's.

The caisson was drawn by six white horses with a seventh as an outrider. Slowly, ever so gently.

"It was a processional," wrote William S. White, who watched from the crowd, "of terrible simplicity and a march too solemn for tears except here and there where someone wept alone. It was a march for all its restrained and slight military display, characterized not by this nor by the thousands of flags that hung limply everywhere but by a mass attitude of unuttered, unmistakable prayer."

As the caisson rolled slowly into view, a radio announcer, Arthur Godfrey, describing the procession to the country, began to cry. To millions of listeners, who thought their reactions were private, his public reaction was a shock.

Mrs. Roosevelt and her family followed the caisson in a closed car. Then came the car bearing President Truman, Wallace, and Byrnes. Truman sat silent, grave, looking straight ahead. Wallace and Byrnes found themselves talking about things Roosevelt had done that they thought foolish; especially, an attempt by Roosevelt to defeat several Congressmen of his own party in Democratic primaries. Harry Hopkins, they agreed, had sold Roosevelt on entering that bitter battle and led him into taking an awful licking.

In the cars behind them rode Cabinet members, Army and Navy leaders, diplomats, White House staff. In one of them, Grace Tully was remembering other homecomings, when she had sat beside the President in his car:

"I would watch the faces of the people as they suddenly recognized him. I would call his attention to a girl on the corner as she waved her arms high in the air, to a man who held his hat aloft, or to an old woman jumping up and down in delight. And he would always wave back or put his hand up to his hat in a salute.

"Frequently during the war years, he would remark about an attractive WAC or WAVE that caught his eye. Women in uniform would recall to his mind the time during the first World War when he was asked to review the Yeomanettes . . . Women in those days did not go in for boyish figures, and a quarter of a century later he would still laugh when he described the sideview of our Navy Women's Corps as he reviewed it in 1917 and 1918.

"Now, on this homecoming, the people on the streets were banked together in stolid or open grief."

The procession turned right into 15th Street beside the White House grounds. The crowds thickened. In a few moments he would be gone from the streets, from the people. The Marine band began to play "Lead Kindly Light." A tall, straight soldier, his back to the crowd, let his rifle slide from his hands as the caisson rolled by. His legs gave way and he melted into an olive drab heap. His face, gashed by his bayonet, was bleeding. The procession turned left into Pennsylvania Avenue. The gate was near. The moments now were few. An elderly Negro woman, sitting on the Pennsylvania Avenue curb, rocked and moaned, "Oh, he's gone. He's gone forever. I loved him so. He's never coming back." At the gate, another woman, half-bowing, half-kneeling, cried, "Oh Lord, he's gone, forever and forever and forever. . . ."

The caisson rolled through the Northwest gate and stopped. On the north lawn, a Navy band played the National Anthem.

President Truman slipped away from the cortege to his office in the West Wing, allowing the mourning family to enter the White House alone. Henry Wallace sprinted across the lawn and, holding his hat to his breast, watched solemnly from under a tree.

A squad of coffin bearers, led by Master Sergeant James W. Powder of Rockford, Illinois, lifted the coffin from the caisson and carried it up the five polished marble steps of the White House and through its narrow front door. Immediately behind it walked Mrs. Roosevelt.

While some were free to give themselves over to the emotions of the hour—to observe, to contemplate, to mourn, to weep—the new President of the United States was not. A world at war was still spinning and Harry S. Truman was at its hub, the man in charge. In his office he received Harry Hopkins, who had flown from his hospital in Minnesota. Always, Hopkins looked run-down and pale. Now he looked ghostly.

"How do you feel, Harry," the President inquired.

"Terrible," Hopkins answered. As always, he was brusque. But as usual, he was to the point.

"I hope," said Truman, "you don't mind my calling you in at this time, but I need to know everything you can tell me about our relations with Russia—all that you know about Stalin and Churchill and the conferences at Cairo, Casablanca, Teheran, and Yalta."

Hopkins, who usually had sat at Roosevelt's side during his critical conferences with these foreign leaders and had undertaken private missions to them in Roosevelt's behalf, was a storehouse of information. He was rarely at a loss for a fact or an incisive characterization. For two hours, he and the new President talked. At lunchtime, Truman ordered trays from the White House kitchen. At the President's desk they nibbled, but most of the food was neglected in favor of their discussion.

"Stalin," said Hopkins, according to Truman's recollection, "is a forthright, rough, tough Russian. He is a Russian partisan through and through, thinking always first of Russia. But he can be talked to frankly."

After Hopkins left, Edward J. Flynn, the New York Democratic leader, was shown into the office. He had come to pay his respects to the new President, he said, but he soon shifted into estimating the political consequences of Roosevelt's death. Truman cut him off, saying that such considerations seemed inappropriate at the moment.

At 2:15, Admiral Leahy and Byrnes came with two messages from Churchill. The first pointed out that advancing Soviet forces on the eastern European front were on the verge of meeting the onrushing Anglo-American Armies of the west. The cable suggested that Truman, Stalin, and Churchill prepare a joint statement to celebrate the occasion. Truman cabled Churchill: "If Stalin agrees, I would be pleased to receive from you for consideration your draft of the message."

The second cable was more troublesome. It was a reply to one Roosevelt had sent Churchill on March 29th, which had proposed launching pilotless bombers from England against large industrial targets in Germany. The bombers, carrying huge explosives, would be guided by remote control and set off by timing devices. Roosevelt had asked for Churchill's consent to the plan. For two weeks Churchill had not answered. Now, finally, his reply explained his hesitation.

Churchill pointed out that the war situation had now turned so sharply in favor of the Allies, that bombing of German cities was no longer of decisive importance. On the other hand, in Greater London thirty thousand civilians had been killed by air onslaught. He frankly feared that the pilotless-bomber plan might invite a suicidal, last-ditch retaliation by German planes. Yet, despite these expressed fears, Churchill's cable concluded: ". . . I leave the decisions entirely in the hands of your military advisers, and we shall make no complaint if misfortune comes to us in consequence."

Truman, after a discussion with Leahy, agreed to postpone the bombing plan.

With each hour, the color of the war in Europe, which only a day earlier the nation's military chiefs had said would take six months to end, was changing. A reporter with the First Army in Germany, Frederick Graham of the New York *Times*, was on this day writing:

"This is a silly war now. No one is sure where the front is. No one is sure where he will meet opposition. No one is sure of anything except that Germans are popping up here and there and they are mighty glad to surrender when there is no German officer to hold a gun at their backs. . . . In Naumburg American soldiers captured a major general who, with 160 men, had put up the defense that had halted us so long. He was utterly disgusted with the war and a bit embarrassed that as a major general in the German army he had only 160 men under his command."

At three o'clock, Truman sent Colonel Harry Vaughan, his old friend who now wore the heavy gold fourragère of

Military Aide to the President, to bring Mrs. Truman and Margaret to the White House. They arrived at 3:30. A few minutes before four, the family left the President's office for the East Room to attend the funeral services of Franklin Roosevelt.

17

"I Saw Him
Real Plain!"

The Boston Symphony Orchestra was playing that afternoon in Carnegie Hall, New York. Sergei Koussevitzky,
the conductor, changed the program he had scheduled and
cancelled the intermission so the concert would end before
four P.M., the time of the funeral service in the White
House. The orchestra played the first movement of Shosta-
kovich's Eighth Symphony and the first two movements of
Beethoven's "Eroica"; then the orchestra and the Harvard
Glee Club joined in a performance of Randall Thompson's "Testament of Freedom." After each piece there was
silence—no applause. The concert had the air of a religious
service. Olin Downes, the music critic, in reviewing it,
voiced the mood of an extraordinary afternoon:

"It was an occasion that far transcended in its significance and atmosphere anything that performances with ex-
clusively artistic objectives could have offered. Yet it was
an achievement of the highest art, an exemplification of the
place that sovereign artists should take in the life of the

world today—by the side of the greatest statesmen and in humanity's cause."

As a comment on a concert to honor a departed man, Downes's review had a peculiarly affirmative, even triumphant ring. It was as though the music had been a tribute not so much to a man as to the spirit of his time—when artists and statesmen, sharecroppers and salesmen, conservatives and liberals, had learned to hold together for a "national purpose." There was a war to win, and a national yearning for a peace to flourish in. And there was a hope that the spirit of the time would stay alive, even if the man who symbolized it had died.

When the concert ended, the crowd poured into 57th Street. Many headed toward Fifth Avenue and the fashionable apartments to the east. The magnificent windows of Fifth Avenue stores were on this day strange. The artifacts of luxury were hidden by long black drapes.

Department stores, cigar stores, shoe shops stayed closed all day. Food stores had closed at two, not to reopen until five. The city's seven hundred motion picture theaters closed until six. The Ringling Brothers Barnum & Bailey circus at Madison Square Garden cancelled its matinee. Newspapers barred all advertising of merchandise.

At five minutes before four a strange thing happened over Manhattan. With fearful suddenness a black cloud collected over the island, causing the streets to grow dark and the people to shudder. Steps quickened, as much from a threat of doom as of rain. A torrent fell and abruptly ended. Then, as quickly as the cloud had come, it disappeared.

On the Lower East Side, at the corner of Rivington and Essex Streets, Mrs. Fannie Kornberg set a radio on the outdoor counter of her store, Harry's Cut Rate Candy Corner, Imported and Domestic. (Mrs. Kornberg's husband, Harry, was in Germany with the Third Army.) A crowd of fifty neighbors gathered among the pickle barrels, waiting for the description of the funeral service to begin. A woman said to her small son, shaking a strict finger as though instructing him, "Not in my lifetime or in yours will we again see such a man." At four o'clock a bell tolled. It was like a signal. The women began to sob. Men moaned, shaking their heads, mumbling ancient prayers. The sounds blended into a strange, prolonged hum.

And then the radio went silent.

Everywhere at four o'clock the radios went silent.

People talking on telephones suddenly said, "Hello, hello, are you there?" Telephone service had momentarily stopped.

In all newspaper offices, the clatter of teletype machines ended. Then slowly, seven letters tapped out:

"S I L E N C E."

Giant newspaper presses groaned to a halt.

In all Western Union offices, the sending of domestic and foreign messages stopped. Operators stood up silently beside their machines.

In the tunnels beneath the city and on elevated tracks over the streets, the New York subway system's 505 trains stopped, whether at stations or not. Passengers looked around puzzled, then folded their newspapers and bowed their heads.

At La Guardia Airport two airplanes that had just landed, but had not yet taxied to the terminal, cut their engines on the runways. Clearances for take-offs were withheld. Other planes circled in the air, their pilots instructed to delay landing except in case of emergency.

At Times Square a traffic policeman, eying the minute hand of a great clock, blew a shrill whistle. Two Broadway trolley cars, moving in opposite directions, jarred to a halt. Their occupants stood up and bared their heads. Near the out-of-town newspaper stand at the foot of Times Tower, a group of men and women dropped to their knees on the wet pavement.

In Boston, fire bells tolled throughout the city. In Chicago, bustling, rambunctious Randolph Street became deathly quiet. In war plants across the land, for exactly two minutes, production was permitted to halt.

At Warm Springs, the people of the village gathered in the Community Building. In the manner of religious testimony, villagers one by one arose to tell a memory of their departed neighbor.

In the White House nearly two hundred funeral guests, who had assembled in a basement reception room, filed upstairs to the East Room. The members of the Cabinet and the Supreme Court were followed by foreign dignitaries: British Foreign Secretary Anthony Eden; Canada's Governor General, the Earl of Athlone; Philippine President Sergio Osmeña; Russian Ambassador Andrei Gromyko; Amir Faisal, the son of King Ibn Saud of Arabia. Bernard Baruch, who had learned of the death in London, had flown back for the funeral of his old friend. Bearded Charles Evans Hughes, the former Chief Justice, sat near General Marshall and Admirals Leahy and King. The Republican governor of New York, Thomas E. Dewey, was joined by a former Republican governor, Harold Stassen of Minnesota. Among the few women were Crown Princess Martha of Norway and Mrs. Woodrow Wilson.

The mourners assembled in rows of gilt chairs. They left the front row, composed of green armchairs, empty. These were for the Roosevelt and Truman families.

The oblong room was lit dimly by three great, cut-glass chandeliers; crimson draperies hung from the windows, huge gilt-framed mirrors from the walls. The walls them-

selves were almost concealed behind ten-foot banks of
lilies and tuberoses. Their scent saturated the humid air
with a clinging sweetness.

In this room Abraham Lincoln, who had been shot
eighty years earlier to the day, had lain in state.

Now, between the Gilbert Stuart portraits of George
and Martha Washington, and between the national colors
and the Presidential flag, on a brown-shrouded bier cen-
tered on a small Oriental rug, lay the closed coffin of
Franklin D. Roosevelt.

Nearby, in the Green Room, the household staff gathered amid an overflow of flowers. In the Blue Room, political associates, too numerous for the East Room to hold,
waited to hear the services through a loudspeaker.

President Truman, his wife and daughter quietly entered the East Room and took their seats in the right front
row. The modest, suddenly burdened man perhaps did not
notice the failure of anyone in the room to stand at the entrance of the President.

Then Mrs. Roosevelt walked down the center aisle, followed by Anna and John Boettiger; Elliott and his wife;
and the wives of James, Franklin, Jr., and John. The assemblage rose until the family was seated. Mrs. Roosevelt,
her face partially hidden by a widow's veil, was wearing a
small gold brooch given to her by her husband as a wed-
ding gift.

The service began with the slow entrance of Episcopal
Bishop Angus Dun, trailed by the Reverend Howard S.
Wilkinson of St. Thomas' Church and the Reverend John
G. McGee of St. John's. Bishop Dun asked for the singing
of "Eternal Father, Strong to Save." Then resonantly, al-
most singing, he delivered the invocation:

"I am the resurrection and the life, saith the Lord: he
that believeth in me, though he were dead, yet shall he
live. . . ."

His assistants alternated in reading from the Psalms. Then the mourners sang a second hymn. Bishop Dun had thought that the request by Mrs. Roosevelt for the singing of "America" was not an altogether agreeable one, and he had obtained her permission to use "Faith of Our Fathers" instead.

The Bishop then offered his prayer. "O God of peace, who hast taught us that in returning and rest we shall be saved . . . remember Thy servant, Franklin Delano, O Lord, according to the favor which Thou bearest unto Thy people. . . .

"O God, from whom every good gift cometh, we thank Thee for the qualities of heart and mind which this Thy servant brought to the service of our nation and our world. For steadfast courage in adversity; for clear vision of dangers to which many shut their eyes; for sympathy with the hungers and fears of common men; for trials met without surrender, and weakness endured without defeat; for unyielding faith in the possibility of a more just and ordered world, delivered from the ancient curse of war; we praise Thee, O God . . . to whom be glory for ever and ever.

"Amen."

When his prayer was finished, Bishop Dun paused and said: "In his First Inaugural Address, the President bore testimony to his own deep faith: '. . . let me assert my firm belief that the only thing we have to fear is fear itself. . . .'

"As that was his first word to us, I am sure he would wish it to be his last; that as we go forward to the tasks in which he has led us, we shall go forward without fear, without fear of the future, without fear of our allies or of our friends, and without fear of our own insufficiency."

The benediction was given at 4:23. Mrs. Roosevelt was first to rise and leave the room. The others filed out slowly.

As President Truman was entering his car he became aware that he had forgotten his hat. Colonel Vaughan, the new military aide, trotted dutifully to the West Wing to fetch it, new gold braid bouncing from his shoulder.

In the White House lobby, Bill Hassett encountered Postmaster General Walker and informed him that Roosevelt had agreed to buy the first sheet of United Nations stamps on his expected arrival at San Francisco. Walker nodded sadly. Then Hassett said it was the last official directive that F.D.R. gave before he died. The Postmaster General squeezed his eyes as though in pain.

Nearby, Harry Hopkins, looking fearfully ill, invited Robert Sherwood and his wife to come home with him. In his Georgetown home, Hopkins, with eyes now gleaming in their sunken sockets, sat in bed and unloosed a nervous monologue. Sherwood later recalled Hopkins' words:

"God damn it, now we've got to get to work on our own. This is where we've really got to begin. We've had it too easy all this time, because we knew he was there, and we had the privilege of being able to get to him. Whatever we thought was the matter with the world, whatever we felt ought to be done about it, we could take our ideas to him, and if he thought there was any merit in them, or if anything that we said got him started on a train of thought of his own, then we'd see him go ahead and do it, and no matter how tremendous it might be or how idealistic he wasn't scared of it. Well—he isn't there now, and we've got to find a way to do things by ourselves.

"I'm pretty sure," Hopkins went on, "that Jimmy Byrnes and Henry Wallace and Harold Ickes are saying right now that they'd be President of the United States today if it weren't for me. But this time I didn't have anything to do with it. I'm certain that the President had made up his mind on Truman long before I got back to the White House last year. . . . People seemed to think that Truman was just suddenly pulled out of a hat—but that wasn't true. The President had had his eye on him for a long time. The Truman Committee record was good— he'd got himself known and liked around the country —and above all he was very popular in the Senate. That was the biggest consideration. The President wanted some-body that would help him when he went up there and asked them to ratify the peace."

Hopkins then told Sherwood that he was going to re-sign at once and that he thought the whole Cabinet should get out except Stimson and Forrestal. "Truman has got to have his own people around him, not Roosevelt's. If we were around, we'd always be looking at him and he'd know we were thinking, 'The *President* wouldn't do it that way!' "

That evening in the East Room, Mrs. Roosevelt re-quested that the casket be opened. She went to it alone and put in a few flowers. Then the casket was sealed for-ever.

At 9:30 P.M. the funeral cortege returned to Union Sta-tion through darkened streets, which again were lined by bayonet-bearing soldiers. Again, people watched in the streets, but this time neither as many nor with such dis-belief.

Two trains waited at the station for the overnight run to Hyde Park. The second of these had been added for members of Congress, diplomats, and additional mourners. The other, the Presidential train, had been lengthened to a string of seventeen cars. It quartered the Truman and Roo-sevelt families, Cabinet members and their wives, the Su-preme Court, and heads of most of the major agencies. Se-cret Service precautions were extraordinary. Never had such an assemblage of government leaders traveled on a single train.

The train was so long and heavy that three times a coupling broke as its engines tried to make it move. The delay cost an hour.

In a car carrying thirteen reporters and five radio men, the heavy mood of the day began to lift and the newsmen slowly became their usual jocular selves. William C. Murphy, Jr., of the Philadelphia *Inquirer* (who was later to become publicity director of the Republican National Committee), growing impatient with the delay, wisecracked to fellow reporters: "The Republicans have always known it would be hard to get Roosevelt out of Washington."

Murphy was asked by one of his colleagues why he didn't get off the train and go home while he still had the chance. The *Inquirer*, he was reminded, would be fed more wire-service material than it could use.

"No sir," Murphy replied. "You guys will be coming back as soon as the old man is buried, but not me. I'm going to sit by his grave for three days and see if he really rises."

Near midnight, the train rumbled quietly into the Baltimore depot. Margaret Truman got out of bed and carefully lifted her shade to look out upon what she describes as "row on row on row of impassive, solemn faces." She got the feeling that it was an intrusion to be looking unseen at the naked grief of others. She lowered the shade. The train stole through the dark city.

Baltimore. Many in the crowd remembered when Roosevelt had come here in 1936 and spoken of the problems of the day as though they were opportunities:

"I, for one, do not believe that the era of the pioneer is at an end; I only believe that the area for pioneering has changed. The period of geographical pioneering is largely finished. But, my friends, the period of social pioneering is

only at its beginning. And make no mistake about it—the same qualities of heroism and faith and vision that were required to bring the forces of Nature into subjection will be required—in even greater measure—to bring under proper control the forces of modern society."

In the Presidential car, Harry Truman was having an intense discussion with James Byrnes as the train left the station. In Car 6, where the Cabinet was, Frank Walker and Henry Wallace each sat gloomily by himself. Henry Morgenthau commented privately to one of his colleagues that Ed Stettinius, the Secretary of State, looked "nervous as a witch." Morgenthau informed the gathering that when he had seen Roosevelt the night before he died, the Boss's hand shook more than usual as he poured a pre-dinner cocktail. But otherwise he looked well and his mind clicked rapidly and accurately as Morgenthau submitted a few matters for clearance. Secretary of the Interior Harold L. Ickes, with a pinched face and tart tongue, was the most talkative in the car, free with uncomplimentary comments about the new President. He bickered with his red-haired wife, saying over and over, "You don't understand the time we're living in." Mrs. Ickes left the car and sat up until 1:30 with Grace Tully. By this time, the train was nearing Philadelphia.

Philadelphia. Roosevelt had come here in 1936 to say that he would run for a second term.

"There is a mysterious cycle in human events. To some generations much is given. Of other generations much is expected. This generation of Americans has a rendezvous with destiny.

"In this world of ours in other lands, there are some people, who, in times past, have lived and fought for

*freedom, and seem to have grown too weary to carry on
the fight. They have sold their heritage of freedom for
the illusion of a living. They have yielded their democracy.*
  *"I believe in my heart that only our success can stir
their ancient hope. They begin to know that here in
America we are waging a great and successful war. It is
not alone a war against want and destitution and economic
demoralization. It is more than that; it is a war for the
survival of democracy. We are fighting to save a great
and precious form of government for ourselves and for
the world."*

The train drew into Pennsylvania Station, New York,
at 4:36 A.M. The platform was heavily guarded. The engines were changed and at 5:00 A.M. the train drew out.
For almost an hour it paused at the Mott Haven railroad
yards in the Bronx. Secret Service men, patrolmen, de-
tectives, and military police formed a broad cordon around
the train, keeping spectators away. Vigilant soldiers manned
submachine guns atop a viaduct at 156th Street. Military
police patroled the streets between Park and Sheridan Ave-
nues and from 156th to 161st Streets.

It was dawn. President Truman, in his drawing room,
was holding an early conference with Secretary Ickes.
Henry Wallace sat in a dining car. A gang of car washers
worked the length of the train. One laborer sloshed a pail
of water against the dining-car window, and Wallace
ducked.

Then the train, as though grudgingly, groaned out of
New York for the last leg of its journey.

New York. It was to the people of this city in 1938 that
Roosevelt said:
  *"If the fires of freedom and civil liberties burn low in
other lands, they must be made brighter in our own.*

"*If in other lands the press and books and literature of all kinds are censored, we must redouble our efforts here to keep them free.*

"*If in other lands the eternal truths of the past are threatened by intolerance we must provide a safe place for their perpetuation.*

"*There may be times when men and women in the turmoil of change lose touch with the civilized gains of centuries of education: but the gains of education are never really lost. Books may be burned and cities sacked, but truth, like the yearning for freedom, lives in the hearts of humble men and women. The ultimate victory of tomorrow is with democracy, and through democracy with education, for no people in all the world can be kept eternally ignorant or eternally enslaved.*"

In the gray of morning farther north along the Hudson, at the tiny town of Garrison, opposite West Point, a man who was a writer for *The New Yorker* posted himself near the railroad track. Another man arrived, accompanied by his small son.

"You've got to remember everything you see today," the father said.

The boy shivered. "It's awfully cold."

Two or three dozen automobiles collected. Their occupants, seeming more excited than sad, stood by the station. A boy in a Mackinaw dashed to the watchman's shack and dashed back, shouting, "Be here in three minutes."

Three minutes went by. No train. A group of Capuchin brothers, bearded, wearing sandals and brown cassocks bound with white cords, arrived. They had walked a mile from their monastery at Glenclyffe.

A woman in the crowd said: "It'll be just terrible if I don't see him."

"They'll slow up when they see us," a man replied.

A plume of white smoke appeared over the trees and the train curved into view. Some men removed their hats. The locomotive pounded by, then car upon car. The last car, with the flag-covered coffin and the military guard, rumbled past and was gone up the track.

"I saw him!" a little girl cried. "I saw him real plain!"

Her mother, embarrassed, said: "You couldn't have seen him. He was sleeping under the American flag."

"I saw him," the girl insisted.

The boy and his father, among the first to come, now started to leave.

"I saw *everything*," the boy said.

"That's good," the father said. "Now make sure you remember."

18

"The River Road"

Captain Francis Resta, leader of the Army Band of the United States Military Academy at West Point, sat in silence as the band bus grunted across the Mid-Hudson Bridge toward Poughkeepsie. Hyde Park was only six miles up the Hudson Valley and he had to make a decision fast.

Then, his face resolute, he lumbered down the aisle to the seat of First Sergeant Mervin Chamberlain. Casting a furtive eye toward a young bugler in the rear, the Captain whispered to the Sergeant: "We can't take a chance on him. Look, he's chewing his fingers off, he's so jumpy. I say let Fisher do it. He's cool, sure of himself. Go tell him."

Sergeant Chamberlain moved down the aisle for a whispered conference with the first chair solo cornetist, Master Sergeant Newell E. Fisher, a chubby, poker-faced Army veteran in his late thirties. Fisher nodded. Chamberlain returned to his seat.

Fisher kept looking out the window, making an effort

not to think about his new assignment. How strange to find himself an actor in a great drama that was so remote two-and-a-half days earlier when his little son had said, "The man in the light house is dead," and his daughter had corrected the boy: "Junior's got it wrong. It said the man in the *White* House is dead."

The band bus stopped at a private siding at the edge of the Roosevelt estate to await the arrival of the funeral train. At 8:40 A.M. the train drew in. As the coffin was lifted through a window of the train, the mighty blast of a cannon rocked the earth. Fifteen seconds later, the violence exploded again. Then again and again, at fifteen-second intervals, twenty-one times in all.

The pallbearers slid the coffin into a hearse that carried it a short distance to the foot of a great bluff below the family homestead. There, the coffin was set to rest on a caisson led by six brown horses. Behind the caisson there followed a seventh brown horse; its head and most of its body was hooded, stirrups turned backward, a sword and upside-down boots hanging from the left stirrup—the symbol of a fallen warrior.

Led by the West Point band in dark blue tunics and light blue trousers with white stripes, the caisson began its climb up a winding, thickly wooded dirt road.

Franklin Delano Roosevelt—making his way, slow and easy, along the road that as a child he had always called "the river road"—was almost home.

At the top of this hill he was born on January 30, 1882. His father had planned the clearing of the trees to make this river road in 1870. A thousand feet to the north, his father had built a boathouse, where in 1890 he had taught young Franklin to row a wherry on the river.

Here Franklin had galloped through the meadows with the sons of Archibald Rogers—Ed, Coleman, and Ray—and cantered on his pony into town on Route 9, except that nobody ever called it anything but the Old Post Road in those days. Here he watched the ways of his father, James, who was an old man when Franklin was still a boy. When the old squire died, Franklin, then eighteen, already had learned to be protective and loyal to the people who came to work on the Roosevelt place. They were not transient help; when they came, they stayed, some for the rest of their lives. Franklin learned to develop a friendly, but decidedly paternal, responsibility for their present and their future. As his experience broadened, this protectiveness and loyalty expanded; one could hear shadings of it years later when he addressed the people of a troubled nation as "My friends . . ." and proceeded to direct the ways for taking care of everyone. Not everyone recognized these shadings, but some of his neighbors in Hyde Park did. He was the country squire, looking after the folks.

He became, like his father, a Democrat among Republican neighbors; he went to Harvard and Columbia and came home to become a lawyer. In 1910, when his friends, the Democrats, needed a good man to run and inevitably be defeated for the State Senate, they asked tall, good-looking, good-voiced, and properly schooled Franklin Roosevelt. Already he had a flair for the dramatic: he campaigned around the district in, of all things, a motor car. He fretted over his first speeches, but it hardly showed through the fine, poised bearing of a country gentleman; only his young wife Eleanor worried, whenever he came to a long pause, whether he would be able to go on.

It was the beginning of the Roosevelt luck. The Democrats won the state by a landslide that year, so heavily that even young Roosevelt in Dutchess County was carried into office. He went to Albany unknown, green, only twenty-eight.

Eleven years later, having served as wartime Assistant

Secretary of the Navy and as his party's candidate for
Vice-President, Roosevelt was felled by polio at Campo-
bello. He returned to Hyde Park, a promising career apparently ended. He began casting about for a project to
help him fight the boredom of recuperating. Old Ben
Haviland, a neighbor (who was now at the top of the hill,
waiting by the open grave), has recalled the time:

"When he was convalescing, his wife would drive him
by my house. I was writing a history then all about Hyde
Park's part in World War I. Roosevelt figured he'd do a
history of the town. He came to me and said, 'Uncle Ben,
they tell me that you know everything about the town's
history.' And I said, 'No, I don't know everything, but I
know some of it.' And we worked together on the history,
sometimes at his house, sometimes at mine."

But Roosevelt, not content with such things as com-
piling a local history, soon responded to the urgings of his
friends and re-entered politics. In less than a decade, he was
Governor of New York. A great depression swept over
America, and a desperate people hopefully made him their
President. A great war came, and they elected him for a
third term, then a fourth.

And now at the top of the hill they were going to bury
him.

The procession climbed through woodlands full of
blooming violets. As in Warm Springs, the birds chirped a
continuing, trilling song. The sun now was bright, the sky
a deep blue. A chill breeze, perfumed by apple blossom,
swept across the Hudson.

The climb was steep. The breath of the marchers came
hard; the band couldn't both climb and play. The brass and
woodwinds stopped playing, but the drummers drummed
a relentless, rhythmic crescendo.

The solemn, winding procession kept rising toward

the waiting grave, bearing the dead as though to a final
view of the woodland, the river, the distant peaks.

*"I see an America where . . . there is no endless chain
of poverty from generation to generation, where impov-
erished farmers and farm hands do not become homeless
wanderers, where monopoly does not make youth a beg-
gar for a job.*

*"I see an America of great cultural and educational op-
portunities for all its people.*

*"I see an America whose rivers and valleys and lakes—
hills and streams and plains—the mountains over our
land and nature's wealth deep under the earth—are pro-
tected as the rightful heritage of all the people . . ."*

At the top of the hill, behind a ten-foot hedge in the
rose garden, William Plog, for fifty years the keeper of
the Roosevelt grounds, made a final inspection of the
empty grave of his employer. The mourners, who had
come to the burying place through the village in automobiles, waited. To the east, the Cabinet, members of the
Congress, government and political friends; to the west,
the Supreme Court and more officials; to the north, Roosevelt's Hyde Park neighbors.

The band, reaching the top of the hill, halted outside
the garden, playing Chopin's "Funeral March." An escort
of West Point cadets in gray uniforms, gold buttons,
white crossed belts, and white gloves, marched rigidly in
two hundred rows of three; to the west of the grave they
formed a solid phalanx.

A voice commanded, "Present—*arms!*"

The coffin, borne by eight servicemen, moved into
the garden.

Mrs. Roosevelt walked behind it, followed by members

of her family. They stopped a few feet before the grave. About fifteen paces behind her stood President Truman and his family, with James Byrnes and Colonel Vaughan.

The band played "Nearer My God to Thee," as through the leafy gateway slowly stepped a young crucifer; behind him walked the aged and frail Reverend George W. Anthony, rector of St. James Episcopal Church of Hyde Park.

Deep, vibrant, cultivated, his voice fought the river breeze:

"Unto Almighty God we commend the soul of our brother departed, and we commit his body to the ground; earth to earth, ashes to ashes, dust to dust . . ."

A lone airplane circling overhead almost buried his words.

". . . unto eternal life, . . . blessed are the dead who die in the Lord . . . Lord, have mercy upon us. Christ, have mercy upon us. Lord, have mercy upon us."

He pronounced the Lord's Prayer. As he spoke the words, Elliott Roosevelt's lips moved silently with his.

The minister raised his thin, sure hand and the soldiers lowered the body slowly into the grave as he intoned:

> Now the laborer's task is o'er;
>   Now the battle day is past;
> Now upon the farther shore
>   Lands the voyager at last.
>   Father, in Thy gracious keeping
>   Leave we now Thy servant sleeping.

A file of West Pointers advanced.

"Atten-*tion!*

"Present *arms!*

"Ready! Aim! *Fire!*"

At the startling shot, Fala, held on a leash by Margaret Suckley, cowered, unloosed a yelp, and rolled over.

"Ready! Aim! *Fire!*"

This time a baby in the rear of the crowd of Hyde Park neighbors began to cry. Its father rushed the child out of the garden.

"Ready! Aim! *Fire!*"

Then the Captain commanding the band nodded ever so slightly.

Sergeant Newell Fisher, first solo cornetist, with sure, slow step, moved forward to the grave. The time was 10:51.

He lifted his silver instrument to his lips, looked slightly upward, and blew the long, mournful finality of taps.

Appendix

A few days after the burial of President Roosevelt a four-page document, penciled by his own hand, was found in the safe in his bedroom at the White House. It was addressed to his oldest son, James, and contained his funeral and burial instructions. The full text of this document follows:

In the event of my death in office as President of the United States I make the following requests:

1. That a service of the utmost simplicity be held in the East Room of the White House, to be attended only by the household, by those in the Executive Office who have been close to me, by the Cabinet and their families and by such other members of the Administrative Branch as have been close to me.

2. That there be no Lying in State anywhere.

3. That the Army have charge of taking the casket to the Rotunda of the Capitol and that immediately at 12 noon a simple service be held there, the Congress, Judiciary and Diplomatic Corps attending. I request that the service last

not more than 20 minutes and that there be only prayers by Rev. Endicott Peabody and two hymns—no speaking. Army in charge all day, to the train.

4. That the funeral train leave for Hyde Park at 1 P.M. arriving there at 8 P.M. and that it be accompanied only by those who are to attend the interment. That the Navy have charge of the train and everything thereafter.

5. That on arrival at Hyde Park the casket be taken to St. James' Church and a simple short service be held, the old neighbors of mine only being asked. Casket to be borne by Marines.

6. That then the casket be taken from the Church to the house, and placed in front of the East fireplace in the big room for the night.

7. That the following morning the interment take place where the sun dial stands in the garden, and that the casket be carried from the house to the garden by men from the place including the Boreel place and the back farms and Valkill Cottage.

8. That the interment be attended only by the family, the Cabinet, the President, the Speaker and not to exceed 2 Senators and 2 Representatives.

9. That a gun-carriage and not a hearse be used throughout.

10. That the casket be of absolute simplicity, dark wood, that the body be not embalmed or hermetically sealed, and that the grave be not lined with brick, cement or stones.

11. That a plain white marble monument no carving or decoration be placed over the grave, east and west as follows:

Length	8 feet
Width	4 feet
Height	3 feet

The whole to be set on a marble base extending 2 feet out beyond the monument all round, but said base not to be more than six inches above the ground.

12. It is my hope that my dear wife will on her death be

buried there also, and that the monument contain no device or inscription except the following on the South side:

FRANKLIN DELANO ROOSEVELT

1882-19-

ANNA ELEANOR ROOSEVELT

1884-19-

13. That only the Rector of St James Church officiate at the interment.

14. That no moving pictures be taken on the place, and only 3 still camera men be allowed at St. James or at the house or garden. 3 Newspaper men only—press associations.

15. That a detail of marines and State Troopers guard the garden, house and grounds for a reasonable time and that the public be not admitted to the place until adequate arrangements can be made.

16. That any period of national mourning be limited to one month.

17. That subsequent care of the garden, house and grounds be arranged substantially in accord with memorandum covering this and enclosed with this.

s/FRANKLIN D. ROOSEVELT

The White House
Dec. 26th 1937

(The memorandum described in the final paragraph has not been found. If it was ever written, it was perhaps destroyed by the President upon the preparation of his will, written in November, 1941, or upon the designation on January 15, 1944—during the President's lifetime—of his house as a national historic site.)

Acknowledgments

The way some people talk, one would think that books describing a single event are something new—a passing literary fad. But they are neither new nor passing. The first in a long line of books of this genre was the book of Genesis. Perhaps the last will be called "The Day Curiosity Died."

Until that final book is written, readers and writers will continue to be curious about the details of certain extraordinary events. They offer a means of stealing experiences from other people's lives to help overcome the limitations of our own.

Perhaps "stealing" is not the right word. It implies that the person from whom the experience was taken was unwilling to give it. Nothing could be less true. While most of us have a natural eagerness to read about the exciting lives of others, those who experience great events seem equally eager to tell about them.

How could this book have been done, for example, if Mrs. Franklin D. Roosevelt had not been willing to suspend her activity in current affairs to submit to a detailed, frank talk about an event long past? Or Grace Tully who, despite the demands on her as Executive Secretary to the Democratic Policy Committee of the Senate, offered to give what is most rare and welcome to any reporter: "as much time as you need." Or William D. Hassett who, surrounded by the F.D.R. mementoes that cover the walls of his Vermont home, plumbed his long and rich memory tirelessly until he was sure I had all I had come to get.

Or Merriman Smith, who took time out from the White House Press Room on a day of international crisis (he had just returned with President Eisenhower from the ill-fated Summit Meeting at Paris) to reminisce at length about the death of an earlier President. Or William D. Simmons, still the chief receptionist at the White House, who talked with me for three-and-a-half hours, never once looking at his watch, interrupting his vivid recollections only to ask—repeatedly, as though he didn't believe it—"How come a young fellow like you in this day and age is interested in Roosevelt?" Or Margaret Suckley, blessed with a photographic memory (appropriately, she is now in charge of the photo collection at the Franklin D. Roosevelt Library at Hyde Park), who helped me draw diagrams of who sat where and who saw what at the time the President collapsed. Or Henry A. Wallace, who read to me (but declined to let me read) from his voluminous personal journal. Or Dewey Long, the White House transportation officer then and now, who patiently struggled with my ignorance of railroading, as we pored over his careful records of the President's funeral train.

Or Lizzie McDuffie, who endured without complaint a hardship I inflicted on no other person I interviewed: the intimidating presence of a tape recorder. (It may please Mrs. McDuffie to know that the tape of her remarkable three-hour interview has been deposited as an historical document at the Roosevelt Library.) Or Hoke S. "Red" Shipp, Executive Housekeeper of the Warm Springs Foundation, who drove me through miles of crisscrossing back roads while I clocked distances (if he thought it was all silly, he never let on), and then wouldn't even let me buy his dinner. Or Minnie Bell Simmons, the present manager of the Warm Springs Hotel, who one night, hearing me ask what Country Captain was like, put that elaborate treat on her dining-room menu—and then no one ordered it but me.

Or Joe Myler of United Press International in Washington, whose feeling for history had inspired him to write a detailed memo of how his office handled the flash, and who lent me his original penciled scrawls of Steve Early's fateful phone message. Or Betsy Tupman Deekens, the former I.N.S. dictation girl, who had written notes that were invaluable to me in describing the newsroom scenes.

And how can I adequately thank Dr. Howard G. Bruenn (now practicing medicine in New York), who would be pleased to forget that he was chosen by fate to perform the sad duty of pronouncing the death of a President—but who told what he remembered with vividness and frankness.

Many others gave their time to tell me what they remembered. There were, among these, Dorothy Brady, Ann Fischer Brinkley, David Brinkley, Mervin Chamberlain, Jonathan Daniels, Laura Delano, Charles W. Ferguson, Mrs. Newell E. Fisher, Johnnie Bell Gates, Louise Hachmeister, W. Averell Harriman, John Holton, Graham Jackson, Dr. Lawrence Jacques, Robert G. Nixon, D. Harold Oliver, C.A. Pless, Nicholas Robbins, John Roosevelt, Harry B. Siegel, Tom Simmons, Haden Snoderly, Rexford G. Tugwell, Mrs. Edwin M. Watson, Victor Weybright, and Claude Wickard.

And there were many newspapermen—supposedly such a hard-boiled lot—who gladly dug into their files, drew meticulous maps and sketches, and searched their memories: Walter Trohan and Laurence Bird of the Chicago *Tribune;* Charles P. Trussell of the New York *Times;* Lyle C. Wilson, Julius Frandsen, and Jerome K. Eldridge of U.P.I.; Arthur Hermann of Gannett Newspapers; Gardner Bridge, J.W. "Bill" Davis, and Bing Miller of A.P.

And there were the countless people—at least I had to stop counting—who told me in interviews, by letter, and by phone where they were and what they were doing when they heard the news. A compilation of their fascinating accounts—only a few of which could be used here—would add up to another book.

If a writer lists the people from whom he succeeded in getting information, he should also confess where he failed. One person, of the many I asked, declined to be interviewed. Madame Elizabeth Shoumatoff has made it her policy not to talk about her unpleasant memories of April 12th. Her recollections, however, were found in reports of a press conference she did give three days after the President's death.

Of all the libraries in which I have had occasion to spend time, none prepared me for the pure joy of working at the Franklin D. Roosevelt Library at Hyde Park. Give a librarian there a list of a dozen books and he brings eighteen—the dozen you asked for and another half-dozen related books that you didn't know about. Mention to an archivist there a vague area of inquiry and he brings a cartful of documents, letters, private notebooks, and original Presidential scribblings. These men seem to care so much about a researcher's success. I am an admirer forever of Herman Kahn, the Library's Director, and of his staff, especially Raymond Corry, Robert L. Jacoby, and Joseph W. Marshall.

To list the published materials that were consulted would be virtually to reproduce the bibliographies already available in any number of excellent books about Roosevelt and his era. Three books, however, were of extraordinary value in yielding narrative accounts that were woven into this story: *Off the Record with F.D.R.:* 1942-1945 (Rutgers University Press) is the title of William D. Hassett's published diary, which he kept whenever he traveled on secret trips with the Boss, such as his final one to Warm Springs; Volume One of the *Memoirs by Harry S. Truman* (Doubleday & Company, Inc.) contains a rewardingly full account of the author's last minutes as Vice-President and first days as President; and Grace Tully's *F.D.R.: My Boss* (Charles Scribner's Sons) is just what a reader would want—a detailed, intimate look at a prominent figure, as his astute and devoted secretary saw him.

Useful material on the events in Warm Springs was provided by A. Merriman Smith's *Thank You, Mr. President:* A White House Notebook (Harper & Brothers), Ruth Stevens' *Hi-Ya Neighbor* (Tupper & Love, Inc.), Michael F. Reilly's *Reilly of the White House* with William J. Slocum (Simon and Schuster, Inc.), Turnley Walker's *Roosevelt and the Warm Springs Story* (A.A. Wyn, Inc.), and Ross T. McIntire's *White House Physician* with George Creel (G.P. Putnam's Sons). I found answers to questions I am not sure I would have dared to ask—about the experiences of the undertakers—in the most specialized trade publication I have ever heard of: *The Southern Funeral Director.*

Two books by Jonathan Daniels—*Frontier on the Potomac* (The Macmillan Co.) and *Man of Independence* (J.B. Lippincott Co.)—contributed to reconstructing the Truman swearing-in ceremony and the opening days of the Truman Administration. A third book by Mr. Daniels *End of Innocence* (J.B. Lippincott Co.), was useful in defining the association between the Roosevelt and Rutherfurd families. The swearing-in scene also drew material from James F. Byrnes's *All in One Lifetime* (Harper & Brothers) and William L. Laurence's *Men and Atoms* (Simon and Schuster, Inc.).

The description of events surrounding the President's funeral was enriched by material in Mary Margaret Truman's *Souvenir* with Margaret Cousins (McGraw-Hill Book Co.), Robert E. Sherwood's *Roosevelt and Hopkins:* An Intimate History (Harper & Brothers), and Edith Helm's *The Captains and the Kings* (G.P. Putnam's Sons).

Experiences of the President's immediate family were found in Eleanor Roosevelt's *This I Remember* (Harper & Brothers) and James Roosevelt's *Affectionately, F.D.R.* with Sidney Shalett (Harcourt, Brace & World). A booklet by Mrs. Roosevelt, *Franklin D. Roosevelt and Hyde Park* (U.S. Government Printing Office, Department of the Interior), offered some interesting details of the President's younger days.

Dwight D. Eisenhower's *Crusade in Europe* (Doubleday & Co., Inc.) and Winston Churchill's *The Second World War,* edited by Denis Kelly (Houghton Mifflin Co.) each told how its author learned the news of the President's death. The receipt of the news in Berlin was covered by Alan Bullock's *Hitler:* A Study in Tyranny (Harper & Brothers).

Of the many newspapers consulted, the New York *Times*

was by far the most helpful, and proved to be most reliable when facts were cross-checked with other sources.

There were ways, other than contributing information, in which help was given. At the Little White House in Warm Springs, which today is a shrine any tourist would profit in visiting, Charles F. Palmer and Charles A. Phelan, Jr., were warmly coöperative. At the White House, Mary Mead of the Press Secretary's staff, graciously arranged whatever tours and interviews I requested. Allen Drury, whose quiet savvy about Washington has become well known, kindly read portions of the manuscript for its accuracy in depicting Capitol Hill folkways. Tadd Fisher was a valuable research aide in Washington. Peter Wyden of the *Saturday Evening Post*, who knows what is behind many closed doors in Washington, helped to pry some of them open. Major Robert F. Prentiss, of the Book and Magazine Branch of the Army Office of Information, saved me from getting lost in the corridors of the Pentagon.

This book would somehow have been completed even if I had not been cheered on by Paul and Naome Walsh, but I don't know how. I hate to think about it.

And the man who painstakingly searched through my manuscript to discover my honorable intentions, then prodded me into living up to them, was Robert Lescher of Holt, Rinehart and Winston. The late Wolcott Gibbs once made the comment to him that an editor's function is "to superimpose grammar on genius." In the preparation of this book, Mr. Lescher superimposed much more upon much less. Louise Waller, also of Holt, Rinehart and Winston, was most self-demanding and patient in the laborious task of verifying factual material.

Now, as for my wife Mildred, true, she boiled the endless pots of coffee and shushed the kids and replaced the light bulbs just as I have read that other writers' wives do. But these are not what I wish to acknowledge here. The important thing she did was to keep acting as though the world were a reasonable place while the unreasonable act of writing a book was being performed right in her own home. To any woman of less fortitude and good cheer than such a task requires, I offer this closing word: Never marry a writer.

Index